FLEETWOOD

M
A
C

FLEETWOOD MAC

M A C

by STEVE CLARKE

PROTEUS BOOKS
LONDON/NEW YORK

PROTEUS BOOKS is an imprint of
The Proteus Publishing Group

United States
PROTEUS PUBLISHING COMPANY, INC.
9, West 57th Street, Suite 4503
New York, NY 10019

distributed by:
CHERRY LANE BOOKS COMPANY, INC.
P.O. Box 430
Port Chester, NY 10573

United Kingdom
PROTEUS BOOKS LIMITED
Bremar House, Sale Place
London W2 1PT

distributed by:
J. M. DENT & SONS (DISTRIBUTION) LIMITED,
Dunhams Lane, Letchworth
Herts. SG6 1LF

ISBN 0 86276 111 5 (paperback)
ISBN 0 86276 112 3 (hardback)

First published in U.S. 1984
First published in U.K. 1984

Photocredits:
Rob Burt Collection; Andre Csillag; Decca: David
Wedgbury; Harry Goodwin; David McGough, John
Paschal/DMI; Barry Plummer; Retna Ltd,; Rex Features;
Ebet Roberts; Joseph Sia; Star File; Barrie Wentzell

Editor: Mike Teasdale

Designed by: Rob Burt
Typeset by: SX Composing Ltd, Rayleigh, Essex
Printed in and Bound in Great Britain
by Blantyre Printing & Binding Co., Glasgow

CONTENTS

BREAKING THE BLUES

*T*he individuals who made up the band that called itself Peter Green's Fleetwood Mac were no strangers to the music business when on a summer's evening in 1967 they made their first public appearance, at the Windsor Jazz & Blues Festival.

The core of this bejeaned quartet, guitarist Green and drummer Mick Fleetwood, had already played side by side with performers who today enjoy an international following. On that day in 1967 Green and Fleetwood mixed backstage with names like Eric Clapton and John Mayall, and others, including Rod Stewart and Ron Wood, still to make their public imprint.

The night's bill-toppers were the year-old Cream, unquestionably the most fashionable band in the land. True to the times, they had broken with straight blues and were astounding audiences everywhere with their dazzling improvisations and innovative approach to material spun originally from the raw skills of black American bluesmen like Albert King and Skip James.

Also on the bill at Windsor was Jeff Beck, like Clapton a maverick guitarist who'd cast aside pure pop for something more adventurous. Another Windsor attraction was the Big Daddy of British Blues, John Mayall, whose band, the Bluesbreakers served as the nearest thing to a training school then operating in British popular music.

The present Mayall band was noted for the precocious skills of its nineteen-year-old guitarist, Mick Taylor, soon to replace Brian Jones in the Rolling Stones. Some months earlier the autocratic Mayall had shrewdly given the spotlight to another gifted guitarist, Peter Green, on the Bluesbreakers' album, *A Hard Road*. Green had followed the Cream-bound Clapton into the hot seat as Mayall's guitarist. And it was largely because of the reputation Green had quickly earned as Clapton's successor that an untried act like Fleetwood Mac could make its public debut in the prestigious atmosphere of Windsor.

Such was Fleetwood Mac's immediate success that a year later the group would be billed above Mayall. For in this short time Fleetwood Mac would establish itself as the paramount force of the late Sixties' British blues boom.

This sudden upsurge in blues on the British pop charts had been gathering momentum since 1966 when the album Clapton made with Mayall, *Bluesbreakers*, surprised everyone by becoming a Top Ten hit. No-one was more astonished than Mayall himself. 'Looking at Melody Maker and seeing the album in the pop charts was all too much for him', says Mike Vernon, record producer and founder of Blue Horizon Records.

Since the Fifties, British musicians such as Alexis Korner and Cyril Davis had attempted to build up an audience for blues in Britain but, faced with the competition of rock, it was an uphill struggle. Rock and roll was custom-built for teenagers. Blues had a history that went back to the first decade of the twentieth century, and post-war adolescents didn't care that the records they bought would never have been made without the blues pioneers of the first half of the century.

Part of the appeal of blues was its cult status. Like folk music, blues had a purity and a folk poetry that convinced those disillusioned with the rapid commercialisation of rock. The commitment and dedication that blues inspired was taken up as a kind of crusade by musicians like Clapton and Mayall; Mayall actually

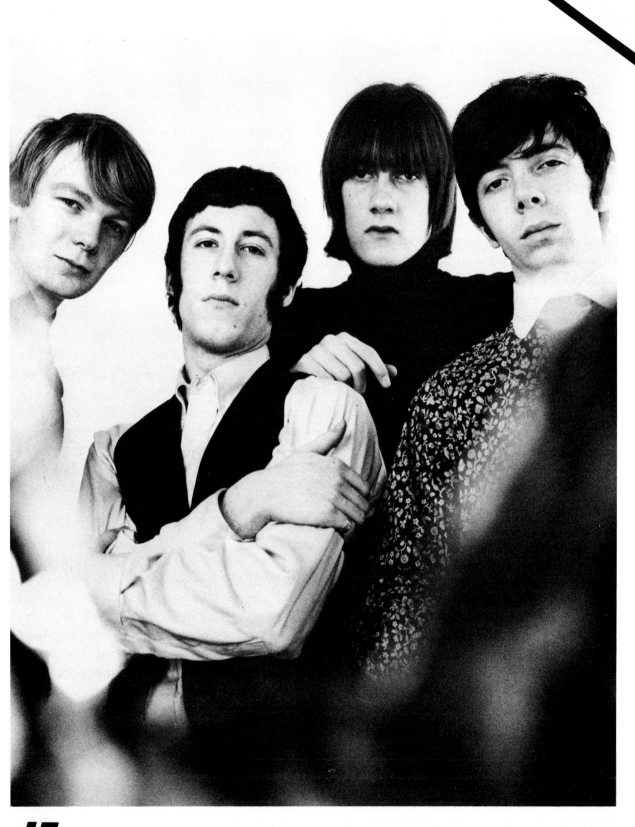

Peter B's Looners; Dave Ambrose, Peter Green, Mick Fleetwood and Peter Bardens

released an album entitled *Crusade* as late as 1967.

The Rolling Stones were the first British group to popularise blues; guitarist Brian Jones and drummer Charlie Watts had both played with Alexis Korner's Blues Incorporated. Significantly, it was a relatively authentic reading of Willie Dixon's *Little Red Rooster* that drove the Stones to the top of the charts in 1964. But as a group, the Stones were never purists and they always mixed material by Muddy Waters and Chuck Berry in their sets. Blues has always been, and still is, a vital ingredient in the Stones' music but it was not until *Bluesbreakers* that blues in all its earnestness came out of the closet and joined its more commercial competitors in the pop charts.

Clapton had joined Mayall after quitting The Yardbirds because in his eyes they had forsaken their commitment to blues for the easy option of recording commercial pop. Mayall was obsessed with blues, self-consciously anti-pop, although his age and sullen dedication were not likely to strike a chord with the nation's teenyboppers.

As a musician his strongest suit was the harmonica but Mayall seemed to play anything and everything; he had moved to London from his native Manchester at the encouragement of Alexis Korner and because of his skills as a multi-instrumentalist was promptly billed as 'Britain's answer to Roland Kirk'. As a singer, Mayall was an acquired taste. He ran his bands on strict autocratic lines, perhaps influenced by his days as a National Serviceman in the Fifties.

With Clapton in his band, Mayall became a top draw on the club circuit. 'It was like the Eric Clapton show, it wasn't John Mayall's Bluesbreakers – there were more people coming along to see Eric', says the group's drummer, Hughie Flint. Fans started to call

Clapton 'God' and fellow musicians gazed nightly from the audience amazed at the ability of the young Clapton.

Mayall knew a good thing when he had one and his next album was billed John Mayall With Eric Clapton. Despite the crude production and dour atmosphere, *Bluesbreakers* was the first classic British blues album, thanks to the skill of Clapton's imaginative and aggressive playing.

One aspiring star musician who listened avidly to *Bluesbreakers* was Peter Green, then playing alongside Mick Fleetwood and keyboard player Peter Bardens (later to form Camel) in the curiously named Peter B's Looners, an instrumental quartet who took their ideas quite blatantly from the Stax house band, Booker T. & The MGs. As Green later said of his infatuation with Clapton: 'I was playing bass semi-professionally. But Clapton gave me a big boost to play lead guitar. I thought "Maybe I can do that too" after hearing him. He was the first big direction I had. I even got a Les Paul guitar because he played one.'

Green was one of three children born (October 29, 1946) to the Greenbaum family in London's working class East End, where there had been a strong Jewish community since the beginning of the century. Like so many would-be rock stars, Green first became acquainted with the guitar during the Fifties' skiffle boom. Inevitably, the next major influence was The Shadows' Hank B. Marvin. Apparently the first blues records Green took any notice of were some old 78s recorded by the late, great city bluesman, Muddy Waters.

Green played with the usual assortment of local dead-end bands before teaming up with Fleetwood in Peter B's Looners. During his three months with the group he recorded one single – *If You Wanna Be Happy* backed by *Jodrell Blues*; the disc proved that Green was a guitarist to keep tabs on. Green stayed

with Fleetwood as Bardens expanded his band to Shotgun Express, taking on board two vocalists, a Liverpudlian called Beryl Marsden and a Londoner, Rod Stewart. Despite this latter asset, Shotgun Express never got beyond the northern soul circuit and Green never had occasion to think twice about his decision to leave the group after just two months for the more secure living afforded by John Mayall's Bluesbreakers.

Green joined Mayall in July 1966. He later said that he was reluctant to accept the bluesman's invitation: 'I always swore I wouldn't take a job with John Mayall. He didn't pay enough.' Apparently an unhappy affair with Marsden influenced Green to throw in his lot with Mayall. Others maintain Green was keen to get himself established in Mayall's outfit. Apparently he had played a handful of gigs with Mayall on an *ad hoc* basis as a stand in for Clapton in the autumn of 1965 when Clapton was 'touring' with his Greek band.

Despite the sublime task of having to fill Clapton's job, Green soon established himself as a guitarist in his own right, despite a tendency to overcompensate for his own lack of confidence, something not helped by the audience's demands to 'Bring back Eric'. Green told a reporter shortly after this baptism of fire: 'They weren't the kind of things which made me play better. They would just bring me down. For a long time with John I wasn't playing at my best, as good as I was able. Only in the last few months with him could I really feel uninhibited.' Mike Vernon has recalled his first impressions of Green: 'He was very quiet and well mannered, rather insignificant really. It wasn't until he started to play that I realised that he was an enormous talent, one that would need perhaps a little edging on but one that could certainly stand up against Eric, which was the unenviable position he found himself in.'

The subsequent album, *A Hard Road*

John Mayall

(1967), reveals Green to be a blues player of finely pitched restraint, in contrast to Clapton's loquacious leads. That Mayall handed over the limelight to Green on three tracks is further indication of the success of the Clapton/Green transfer; Green sings on his own song, *The Same Way* and contributes two instrumentals, including another of his own numbers, *The Supernatural*. This was unquestionably the high spot of the entire album, and it showed Green's gift for carefully understated melodies. The tune came from the same

seam that would give rise to *Albatross*, Fleetwood Mac's first major hit.

Two months after *A Hard Road* was released in Britain in February 1967, the Mayall band underwent another convulsion. Nothing unusual in that, except that this time the line-up now read: John Mayall (keyboard, vocals, harp), Peter Green (guitar, vocals), Mick Fleetwood (drums) and John McVie (bass). In other words, Fleetwood had joined his erstwhile colleague Green, and the nucleus that would form Fleetwood Mac was now complete.

This version of the Bluesbreakers would last precisely two months.

The story of how John McVie, aged seventeen, joined John Mayall has been told so often that it has become almost legendary. The taciturn bassist enrolled with Mayall in the winter of 1963 when Mayall was still making a living as a graphic artist and McVie had begun a career as a lowly civil servant. The thirty-year-old Mayall knew just about all there was to know about blues. McVie knew nothing. His only experience was playing in one of the thousands of groups that then existed in Britain whose *raison d'etre* was to emulate the Shadows and their fancy footwork. McVie remembers his baptism of fire with Mayall: 'Mayall just gave me a pile of records and asked me to listen to them and try and grasp the style and feeling. The first gig I did with him was at The White Hart in Acton . . . he said "OK, let's try a 12 bar in C", and I had to ask him what he meant. He just told me to follow the chords, and over the months I began to learn what the blues was all about.'

McVie and Mayall saw off many a guitarist and drummer until Clapton joined the Bluesbreakers in 1965, and on at least one occasion McVie himself was told to pick up his cards, whereupon Mayall enlisted Jack Bruce. McVie's weakness was the bottle, one of several problems that arose when Mayall and Clapton recorded *Bluesbreakers*. According to Mike Vernon, it was a vice that most of the time McVie could cope with: 'It was a problem he seemed to manage to handle when it was really necessary. Mayall knew of his talents as a bass player and he wasn't about to remove him from the outfit'.

Whatever, McVie was the last of the Fleetwood Mac trio to leave Mayall's wing and the group's Windsor debut featured Bob Brunning on bass; the latter was in the band purely on the understanding that he would relinquish his position once McVie finally made up his mind to leave Mayall. As Fleetwood has said: 'John was on a weekly wage and didn't want to rock the boat – but we kept on at him to join Fleetwood Mac and eventually he agreed.'

On Green's departure, Mayall had revamped the band to include a two piece horn section, a move which McVie soon began to resent: 'I thought that Mayall was getting too jazzy . . . We were doing a gig in Norwich, and we did a sound check, working some arrangements out – this was when I was still a very hard-core blues addict, with the "There's nothing outside of the blues" attitude. So one of the horn players asked, "What kind of solo do you want in this section?" And I'll always remember, John said, "Oh, just play free-form". I thought to myself, "OK, that's it". We used to do two sets, so during the interval I went out and phoned up Greenie and said, "Hey, you need a bass player?"'

****

It is glib but nonetheless tempting to speculate that Mick Fleetwood's upbringing left him with qualities of leadership and discipline that in years to come he would need to steer Fleetwood Mac from the edge of commercial oblivion to superstar status. Born on June 24th 1947, the son of an officer in the RAF, Fleetwood spend much of his early childhood outside England; he was in Egypt with his family during the Suez crisis in 1956 and later lived in Norway where his father was on the NATO pay-roll.

He had the dubious benefit of an English public school education – at King's School, Sherborne – where he discovered a liking for acting and fencing, and the vicarious pleasures of flicking through drum catalogues. In fact, Fleetwood was never to have any career other than that of a rock musician.

The way he tells it he was fifteen when by a stroke of luck a neighbour, Peter Bardens, asked him to join his rhythm & blues group, The Cheynes, described as 'Britain's Most Exciting Rhythm & Blues Sound'. Fleetwood was indifferently employed at one of London's most fashionable department stores, Liberty and accepted Bardens' invitation gladly. Thus began a career of sorts that was four years later to take him to the Bluesbreakers. In between working with The Cheynes and getting acquainted with Green in the aforementioned Shotgun Express, Fleetwood also drummed briefly with the Bo Street Runners, a nondescript outfit whose victory in a television (Ready, Steady, Go!) beat contest failed to lift them from obscurity.

Fleetwood was out of work when, in the spring of 1967, Mayall invited him to replace Aynsley Dunbar, who'd quit to join Jeff Beck's group. Despite the rapport he'd established with Green in Shotgun Express he was surprised at being asked to join Mayall: 'It was never a serious long term venture in my mind, which was just as well, because I was asked to leave after a month.' Mayall over a period of time had learnt to live with McVie's lack of sobriety but having two barflies in tow was too much for the band leader.

Short though Fleetwood's stay was, it gave the trio (Fleetwood, McVie and Green) the time to create a sort of bond in the recording studio, including one single *Double Trouble* and an instrumental recorded without Mayall entitled *Fleetwood Mac*; the track later surfaced on *The Original Fleetwood Mac* in 1971 and was not released at the time.

It is still unclear who came up with the idea of forming Fleetwood Mac, although Green seems the most likely bet. Whatever was to happen in the future, at that time the guitarist had no shortage of ego. As

Fleetwood said years later: 'Pete was very ambitious when he started, maybe overly so. He was intent on making it, this "I'll show you" thing, which I could never understand'.

Yet there are those who suggest that

John Mayall's Bluesbreakers; 1966 (left to right) John Mayall, Eric Clapton, John McVie and Hughie Flint

when Green quit the Bluesbreakers in May 1967, he was not at all certain about his future and weighed up various options, including going to Chicago to play with the black blues musicians who were then his inspiration.

Producer Mike Vernon, however, thinks that Green, together with Fleetwood and McVie had been planning to walk out from the Bluesbreakers for some time. There are even those who contend that Mayall actually

encouraged the trio to go it alone. As Mayall's 1968 album *Bare Wires* shows, even he was not immune to the musical upheavals that were taking place in popular music on both sides of the Atlantic in 1967 as jazz and folk exerted an influence on rock and blues.

Peter Green's Fleetwood Mac, however, was formed initially to play the blues and nothing but the blues. And at Windsor on that summer's evening in 1967 the audience was introduced to one important new name within the new group – the diminutive Jeremy Spencer who carried a torch for the late Mississippi bluesman, Elmore James.

The youngest member of Fleetwood Mac, Spencer (born July 4, 1948) was discovered by Vernon on one of his talent scouting expeditions to Birmingham. The guitarist had written to Vernon 'waffling on continually about Elmore James and Homesick James Williamson', asking him to see his band, the Levi Set Blues Group. Vernon obliged although he could see no future for the band, but immediately took a shine to the elfin Spencer: 'Jeremy really blew me away. He was on the short side, with a flock of curly hair, not unlike Peter's, and he played slide on this large, F-hole semi-acoustic with a pick up. He was playing Elmore James songs – he even sang like Elmore James.'

Vernon arranged for Spencer to visit Green while the latter was playing a Bluesbreakers gig in Birmingham. It was shortly afterwards that Green, Fleetwood, Spencer and the soon-to-go Bob Brunning began rehearsals for Windsor. It is significant that despite Green's apparent confidence, he felt the need to include another guitarist in the line-up. Even at this stage Green was apparently preoccupied with not wanting to become a superstar guitarist à la Clapton. As the next eighteen months were to show, Green was all set for just that kind of acclaim.

A FISTFUL OF HITS

*P*eter Green's Fleetwood Mac was released on February 24, 1968. It was an immediate hit in the British album charts where it held firm well into the summer. The following year the group sold more records in Britain than the Beatles or the Rolling Stones, such was the effect of *Albatross* and its immediate successors, *Man Of The World* and *Oh Well*.

By this time Green's name had been dropped from the mast-head but Fleetwood Mac's success was of the kind that made it impossible for Green to avoid the fact that he had now been elevated in the public mind to Guitar Hero Extraordinaire.

These were heady days for pop and youth culture generally. After *Sgt. Pepper* the Beatles had established themselves as artists in their own right. The sordid death of Brian Jones had cleared the air for the Stones to re-discover their roots, no doubt influenced by the resurgence and unprecedented popularity of blues in the pop charts.

Stunned by the success of Fleetwood Mac, record companies were signing up blues bands with characteristic promiscuity. Several of the better acts like Chicken Shack, Savoy Brown, Ten Years After and particularly Free, are still remembered today. Jethro Tull was another group which launched itself on the crest of this particularly British wave, Canned Heat was a notable American exception. In many ways the Blues Project and the Paul Butterfield Blues Band were ahead of their time in 1965-6 yet too late to exploit the buoyant British market. Even the Beatles felt the need to include a frenzied send-up of the phenomenon with *Yer Blues* on the *White Album*.

While Fleetwood Mac set the pace for the late Sixties British Blues Boom, much of

the credit for this renewed interest in blues must go to their producer, Mike Vernon. For some years Vernon had been laying the groundwork for the commercial success of blues in Britain. In 1964 he was involved with

his brother Richard and another blues freak, Neil Slaven in publishing R&B Monthly, which quickly became something of a bible in R&B circles. When he first met McVie, Green and Fleetwood he was working as a staff producer at Decca Records which, along with EMI, had the majority of the British record industry to itself.

In the Sixties, Decca let many a good opportunity slide through its fingers, not

least the celebrated refusal to take up a
contract with the Beatles. Vernon was unable
to exploit his passion for the blues at Decca
until the music had proved itself in
unquestionable commercial terms.
Undaunted, he formed his own label while
retaining his job at Decca. This small
independent label started off life as Purdah
Records, but by the time Fleetwood Mac had
emerged it had changed its name to Blue
Horizon.

The group gave Vernon the opportunity
he had been looking for to expand Blue
Horizon from a cult label into something
more commercial. So it was with Fleetwood
Mac that Blue Horizon 'took a big step
forward' into being a major label.
Significantly, Decca, which Vernon had
approached for a distribution and pressing
deal, refused to give Blue Horizon the label
identity it needed, and instead a contract
was signed with CBS Records.

For Fleetwood Mac, Blue Horizon had the
advantage of containing someone the
individuals in the band knew and respected,
while it also had the right kind of image the
band needed to assert its ethnic credibility.
Fleetwood Mac's early records were
launched in an atmosphere of purist fervour.
Typically, their first single, Elmore James' *I
Believe My Time Ain't Long*, performed
inevitably by Spencer, was true to its roots,
whilst also showing that the band didn't take
themselves quite as seriously as Mayall had
done.

On this recorded debut Green takes a
back seat providing harmonica breaks as
Spencer hogs the limelight with his
impersonation of the sort of slide guitar
sounds that were originally laid down in
Chess Records' Chicago studios a decade
earlier. At the time Green went on record as
saying: 'There were a million groups making
a mockery of the blues. And a million
guitarists playing as fast as they could and

calling it blues. I didn't want the music
messed about. I was possessive about it'.

Peter Green's Fleetwood Mac, like the
single that went before it, illustrates the
depth of Green's convictions right down to
the carefully studied blues appeal of the
cover art. Or was Green just providing
record company hype in statements like the
above? As subsequent records show, Green
did not restrict himself for long to blues
structures, and as Mick Fleetwood later said:
'I think the musical rules of the blues only
appealed to Pete as an avenue to other
things he could express himself through'.

Green was an instinctive musician who
brought genuine emotional commitment to
his music which he then attempted to
rationalise to interviewers by saying things
like the above quote. Blues suited Green
down to the soles of his scuffed sneakers
because it was raw, emotional music, free of
commercial pollution. It allowed him to
indulge his melancholy emotions. In other
words, Green was well suited
temperamentally to play the blues.

Green and Spencer shared out the
credits between them on *Peter Green's
Fleetwood Mac*. Contrary to popular belief,
Green plays more harp than he does lead
guitar on the album. For guitar freaks,
Green's skills are amply showcased on two
cuts – *Merry-Go-Round*, an archetypal slow
blues, with Green's aching leads sounding
more like B. B. King than the maestro himself,
and *I Loved Another Woman*, a Santana-
esque blues with lots of chilling reverb on
the guitar.

Meanwhile, Spencer dusted off his
Elmore James' licks with an affection and
gusto only he could have provided. The
bull's eye was Spencer's reworking of James'
saucy *Shake Your Honeymaker* on which
the redoubtable rhythm section of
Fleetwood and McVie prove they can really
swing with the best. It's clear why the song

became such an onstage favourite. Elsewhere the Boy Wonder plundered the songbooks of Sonny Boy Williamson and Robert Johnson.

Fleetwood Mac and producer Vernon polished off twelve of the thirteen tracks in just three days (*Long Grey Mare* was recorded while Brunning was still on bass), bucking the trend set by the Beatles marathon sessions for *Sgt. Pepper*.

It was just one month after the release of the album that Fleetwood Mac released their first classic single, Peter Green's *Black Magic Woman*. Even though the long player was still high on the British charts, *Black Magic Woman* failed to reap its just deserts. Over two years would have to elapse before the song became a worldwide hit, recorded not by Fleetwood Mac but by Santana, who, it must be said, get nowhere near the emotional impact of the original.

Technically, *Black Magic Woman* is a blues but this time round Green and his colleagues attack the music like rock musicians. To describe *Black Magic Woman* as Peter Green's vehicle is not to down-grade the contribution of Fleetwood's exotic tomtom playing, but really the record belongs to Green, vocally and as a guitarist of rare artistry. Green's immaculate taste and timing dominate a truly great record.

With hindsight it's possible to explain the record's lack of success by saying that the band's fans were not yet ready for something as sophisticated, compared to the rough and ready approach of the album. Ironically, it was Fleetwood Mac's next single, the perfectly restrained blues with strings, *Need Your Love So Bad* that got the group into the British singles charts for the first time, however briefly.

Green has claimed that B. B. King was

never a major influence on his playing, but actions, as they say, speak louder than words. He discovered this song not by hearing the original version by its composer Little Willie John but by listening to a live rendering recorded by . . . B. B. King. Moreover, the decision to use strings on *Need Your Love So Bad* was doubtlessly influenced by King's *The Thrill Is Gone*. Which is not to detract from the excellence of this very fine record, since the enterprise was so obviously undertaken with great respect for the source of its inspiration. And as Vernon says: 'Peter wasn't conscious of playing a solo and realizing it sounded like B. B. King or someone. He didn't even listen to records very much'.

Coming after two excellent singles, Fleetwood Mac's second album, *Mr Wonderful* was a disappointment. Drafting

in a four piece horn section, Duster Bennett on harmonica and Christine Perfect (soon to be McVie) on piano, the band apparently went out of its way to achieve authenticity. Vernon remembers: 'Jeremy of course was very keen on re-creating the strict Elmore James sound, which was very hard to do, because we didn't really know what went into the original. But Mike Ross, the engineer, and I spent quite a lot of time manouvering amps and microphones to try and get that authentic sound. The horns weren't perfectly in tune, which is synonymous with a lot of the Chicago blues records, and they weren't always in time, either'.

And that wasn't the half of it. As a band Fleetwood Mac sound top heavy and indifferent to the material, once again a mixture of originals and blues standards,

though this time with far more of the former. Whether by accident or design, the mix is muddy and not even Green's talents could move the proceedings out of the doldrums. Had Fleetwood Mac lost direction so early in their career? Their fans didn't seem to notice the album's shortcomings and in Britain *Mr Wonderful* joined its predecessor in the album charts.

For a band which months earlier had been declaring its allegiance to the blues, *Mr Wonderful* was a bizarre record. By this time Fleetwood Mac had achieved a certain notoriety for their ribald stage shows. London's famed Marquee Club banned Fleetwood Mac from the premises after an incident on stage when Fleetwood and Spencer appeared before the audience with all manner of sex aids including condoms filled with beer. The management at the

Marquee wasn't the only club to take offence at the group's risqué sense of humour and liberal use of four letter words. Green was quoted as saying: 'A lot of people don't want to know us because we're so ragged and use bad language on stage. If I want to say fuck then I will, because if I say it normally in my speech then I'm going to say it on stage too – until I get arrested for it'.

The cover art for *Mr Wonderful* had caused CBS (Blue Horizon's UK distributor) anxiety, and the original idea was dropped for a photograph of a crazed and emaciated Fleetwood, naked except for some foliage, itself hardly the epitome of good taste. The band initially wanted to call *Mr Wonderful*, *A Good Length* but CBS demurred, realising that the title was not intended as merely a reference to the drummer's considerable height.

The Melody Maker Awards; 1969 (left to right) John McVie, Danny Kirwan, Jeremy Spencer, Mick Fleetwood, Peter Green

It seems fair to surmise that after a year together Fleetwood Mac was suffering from an identity crisis. They had a captive and committed audience. They'd sold a lot of albums, especially for a group which played Chicago style blues with virtually no concessions to commerciality. But major success still eluded them.

In August 1968 Fleetwood Mac announced that it was adding another guitarist to the band, Danny Kirwan. Green

and Fleetwood had discovered the eighteen-year-old Kirwan playing in a Brixton pub with his trio, Boilerhouse. They were impressed with Kirwan but had serious doubts about the group's rhythm section. Nevertheless Boilerhouse was booked into the Blue Horizon Club at Battersea where Mike Vernon got the chance to scrutinize Kirwan. He was immediately impressed: 'He had a guitar style that wasn't like anyone else I'd heard in England. It reminded me of

Lowell Fulson – there was a certain vibrato in the finger work that was quite unusual. And he really had a nice melodious voice'.

Green persuaded Kirwan to part company with the rest of Boilerhouse and he attempted to find new musicians for Kirwan to work with. When none were found, he was asked to join Fleetwood Mac. Kirwan made his recorded debut with the band on the B side of their next single. The new recruit, like Spencer before, was immediately given a platform to demonstrate his talent, and the B side, a melodic jazzy instrumental written by Kirwan and entitled *Jigsaw Puzzle Blues*, was indeed worthy of attention. At the time, however, the public was more fascinated with the record's A side – *Albatross*.

Released in England in late November, *Albatross* was to make Fleetwood Mac a household name in their own country by Christmas. Rarely has a single record so affected the way the public perceives a band. Nowadays critics, with more than a hint of contempt, would define *Albatross* as adult orientated rock, or, less politely still, as MOR (middle of the road) rock. In late 1968 the fans who treasured their copies of *Peter Green's Fleetwood Mac* and *Mr. Wonderful* were quick to accuse their blues heroes of 'selling out' to the demands of the pop market. To which Green retorted in self defence: '*Albatross* is my baby. It will be around when I'm dead.'

Hindsight has made it clear that there was something to Green's rhetoric. In the fifteen or so years since it was originally released, the record has been played so often and sold so many records everywhere it could possibly sell them, that it has become a sort of cliché. When re-released in Britain five years later in 1973 Albatross once again sailed effortlessly to the top of the charts. Its familiarity is such that it is redundant to attempt to describe the record. What needs to be said here is that *Albatross*'s

immaculate mellifluence made it irresistable to all types of record buyers, including those proud to call themselves Fleetwood Mac afficianados, provided they were not blinded by its latent commerciality.

Had the blues purists used their heads they would have realised that *Albatross* – while not a bar stomping blues – was not the commercial aberration they took it for. Its roots were easily discernible in another of Green's haunting instrumentals, *The Supernatural*, from the *Hard Road* album. Moreover, *Albatross* did not deviate from Green's belief in never playing a cluster of notes when one or two could do the trick more effectively. At the end of the day *Albatross* has the authentic feel of the blues. Otherwise it might have sounded like *Mantovani Plays Electric Guitar*.

Apart from their earliest days together, Fleetwood Mac was always more than just a blues band. Green had always said the right things about his apparent devotion to the music, something that helped create Fleetwood Mac's image. Now it was becoming clear that Green had a much broader musical vision, that stretched beyond a succession of twelve bar shuffles. Earlier in the year Green acknowledged that by including rock 'n' roll numbers in the sets, Fleetwood Mac was deliberately playing to the gallery. He said: 'I've always liked rock, and it's a pity in a way that everyone is going on about the rock thing because it seems as though we're just being "in". Actually I've always wanted to do this kind of thing on stage – but it doesn't mean we'll be neglecting the blues. We're still doing the same kind of numbers as we always did – but I'm playing more to the audience nowadays.'

The follow-up to *Albatross*, *Man Of The World* backed by a B side that quite blatantly exploited Fleetwood Mac's fondness for rock, *Somebody's Gonna Get Their Head Kicked In Tonight*, confirmed Green's

The recording of Blues Jam At Chess. Below: (left to right)
Danny Kirwan, John McVie, Peter Green. Right: Otis
Spann adds a spark to the proceedings.

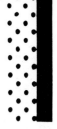

desire to innovate. But before the record was
released Fleetwood Mac saw the new year
in by making a pilgrimage to Marshall
Chess's Chicago Studios where they teamed
up with various local bluesmen to record
four sides of invigorating blues.

The recording was completed in forty-
eight hours and the twenty-two tracks of
original and traditional material feature
various line-ups, including Willie Dixon,
Walter 'Shakey' Horton and Otis Spann.
McVie has complained about the
patronising attitude of the black musicians to
Fleetwood Mac but none of this surfaces on
the record, and Green's undisguised
pleasure at working in Chicago with the

musicians he admires comes through
loudest: 'I didn't so much want to play with
the bluesmen as to hear *them* play. But once
we got going, I didn't care what they thought
of me. I was just happy to be playing', he has
said.

By the time *Blues Jam At Chess* was
released in December 1969 Fleetwood Mac
had ceased to exist in the public's
perception as a straight blues band. Green
was unnecessarily defensive about the
record: 'The bulk of our fans won't like it
because a lot of the blues fans have dropped
us, like they do, because we've been on
television and had hits.' In fact, the album
says it all about Fleetwood Mac's quality as a

29

Danny Kirwan jams with Honey Boy Edwards, Willie Dixon and an almost invisible Mick Fleetwood

blues group. As *Man Of The World* and *Oh Well* suggest, *Blues Jam* was to be the last blues album the group recorded.

Man Of The World was another major British hit for Fleetwood Mac, despite its apparent uncommerciality. That Fleetwood Mac could get to Number Two in the pop

charts with a record like this said a lot about how popular the group now were. Months in the making, it's a meticulously crafted record with a similar down-beat feel to *Albatross*. It makes the impact the sheer depth of feeling Green expresses, both through his anguished guitar playing and the

heartfelt lyrics. *Man Of The World* was the first public sign that Green was disenchanted by his experience as a rock star. It was a theme he would return to more than once in the following months.

In bold contrast to Green's explicit introspection, the B side sees Spencer belting out an hilarious parody of the kind of Fifties' rock 'n' roll he adored. For this vigorous workout Fleetwood Mac adopted the cheeky *nom de plume*, Earl Vince & The Valiants. It was the kind of fare Spencer injected regular into a Fleetwood Mac performance, greasing back his hair and donning a gold lame suit to work the audience into an instant frenzy. Green's malaise had not diminished Fleetwood Mac's sense of humour.

The single was the group's first record not to be released by Blue Horizon. After *Albatross* Fleetwood Mac were the kind of act that every record label wanted to have on their books. Coincidentally the group's contract with Blue Horizon expired at this time. That they did not re-sign to Vernon's largely specialist label was something that

Green has said he didn't altogether approve of: 'I was the last one to agree to leave Blue Horizon. I was quite happy there, and I didn't like leaving just for more money. I said to the other guys, "Watch out, there'll be a comeback from this"'.

As so often happens when large sums of money are at stake in the music business, the break with Vernon was not entirely harmonious. He had spent many hours producing *Man Of The World* but his name is conspicuously absent from the record's

credits. In Britain *Man Of The World* came out on Immediate Records, a relatively new label formed by the entrepreneur who'd introduced the Rolling Stones to the world, Andrew Loog Oldham.

For reasons that are unclear Fleetwood Mac's relationship with Immediate was short-lived. At one time it was reported that the group were close to signing with the Beatles' Apple Records. Fleetwood Mac's manager Clifford Davis told the press: 'The Beatles have heard the new album and have been very friendly with us lately. We may sign with Apple if we can get a reasonable deal, but we are an independent team – we write, produce and record – so we may conceivably form our own label'.

Wisely, Fleetwood Mac did not sign to Apple, but instead took out a contract with the American giant, Warner-Reprise, for whom they still record today. The band's first release on Reprise was the *Then Play On* album, released in the autumn of 1969 and originally entitled *Bread & Kunny*. It was to be Peter Green's last album with Fleetwood Mac.

GREEN GOES UNDER

For those who looked carefully, *Then Play On* showed all the signs of Fleetwood Mac's imminent crisis. It has its moments but overall is a confused offering with only Green's anguish providing any kind of coherent thread. Years later Mick Fleetwood admitted that the band 'didn't have an exact concept' of what they were going to do for their third album. Making another blues album was out of the question, which stopped Jeremy Spencer once again playing homage to the Mississippi Marvel, Elmore James.

Spencer's Elmore James impersonations had shored up Fleetwood Mac's two previous albums. For the third, he was strapped for ideas. 'I had no inspiration . . . couldn't think of anything new. I was just doing Elmore James and I just couldn't think of anything else. There was nothing for me to really sing about anymore', Spencer later confessed. As a result, Spencer appears in name only on *Then Play On*. Originally his contribution was to take the form of a bonus EP (extended play) devoted to his rock 'n' roll parodies but the idea failed to materialise in spite of Mike Vernon spending valuable recording time on the project.

With Spencer out of the proceedings, it was up to Green and Kirwan to furnish the long player with material. Ironically, it was new boy Kirwan who had to shoulder the majority of the album's songwriting. Green wrote five of the record's twelve songs but at least one of Green's compositions, *Under Way*, is merely an *Albatross*-like echo culled from a three hour studio improvisation. This jam also provided the two instrumentals, *Fighting For Madge* and *Searching For Madge* (Madge was a Fleetwood Mac devotee from Darlington), credited respectively to Fleetwood and McVie. *Show-Biz Blues* and *Rattlesnake*

Shake were carefully grafted Green songs.

Kirwan's gifts as a guitarist had already been confirmed on *Jigsaw Puzzle Blues*, the B-side of *Albatross*. On *Then Play On* the listener is again left in no doubt about the wise choice Green had made in drafting this new musician into Fleetwood Mac. The opening cut, *Coming Your Way*, leaves

ample proof of Kirwan's fretboard finesse as he spars energetically with his patron. But to throw him in at the deep end by giving the boy half an album to write was courting trouble. In contrast to Green's muscular paeans to disaffection, sexual (*Rattlesnake Shake*) and spiritual (*Show-Biz Blues*), Kirwan's weak-kneed whimsy was not particularly effective in anything other than a wet, wimpy way. His *When You Say* (later recorded by John McVie's wife, Christine Perfect, as she was then known) is pretty but in need of crisp edit. Which is more than can be said of the slight, *One Sunny Day* and *Although The Sun Is Shining*. Kirwan possessed an immature talent that needed nurturing. Green's habit of constantly down-grading himself placed the stripling in circumstances he wasn't yet ready for. As Fleetwood said later: 'It was another example of Pete trying to steer people away from the big Peter Green image.'

During this stage in Fleetwood Mac's career it was not uncommon for Green to come out with statements like: 'Danny and Jeremy do much more writing than I do. I just write the odd song here and there.' Green's output in the band's brief two year history was never prolific but his songs were of a quality that neither Spencer nor Kirwan could even begin to match. Not that Spencer had ever had an original musical idea. Following on from *Man Of The World*, Green's predominant mood, as expressed in his songs on *Then Play On*, was one of disenchanted introspection. The up-tempo country blues, *Show-Biz Blues*, reiterated the sentiments of *Man Of The World* but where Green had once sounded resigned, this newer song revealed a bitterness towards those who rushed to hero worship him. Here, Green's spiritual discontent with material success led him, perhaps inevitably, to God: 'If I needed someone I would take you home with me/I don't need

anybody but Him and me.' This newly articulated 'faith' is repeated in the sombre *Closing My Eyes*, and in the next Fleetwood Mac single, Green's masterly *Oh Well Parts 1 and 2* where he refers specifically to his relationship with God.

Without wishing in anyway to question Green's sincerity, it should be recalled that during the late Sixties it became fashionable for rock stars to suddenly find favour with various kinds of religious belief, often of an Oriental kind. Inevitably it was the Beatles who were the first to dabble in this area. They, of course, had their well-documented fling with the Maharishi, though with George Harrison the interest in Eastern mysticism went considerably deeper than it did for the other three Beatles for whom it appeared to be little more than an overnight sensation. It is Harrison's *My Sweet Lord* (1971) that best sums up this spate of 'God-rock'. Blind Faith's *In The Presence Of The Lord* (1969) is another example of a rock musician (Eric Clapton) pinning his hopes to a new found religious faith when the predictable cycle of sensual pleasures, notably hallucinogenic drugs, began to sour, however fleetingly.

Green too had experimented with mind expanding drugs. Years later he told a reporter about an experience with mescalin during an American tour: 'I was touring America and one night took the drug at a party. Everyone else went to bed but I had this vision of a man watching TV. There were pictures of starving people in Biafra on the screen. I remember thinking "We can get TV cameras there, but we can't get them food". And then the man in my dress got up, ready to go to bed, and just switched off the TV set. I realised I was at a crossoads. I had more money than I needed.'

The incident probably occurred during Fleetwood Mac's second American tour, at the end of 1969. Despite its lack of direction, *Then Play On* was the first Fleetwood Mac album to sell over 100,000 copies in the States. Its blatant rock characteristics were more to the taste of Stateside audience than the relatively traditional blues of the band's earlier work. In Britain *Then Play On* got mixed reviews but sold well without creating the impact of *Peter Green's Fleetwood Mac*. That was left to *Oh Well*, the sales of which were enough to ensure that Fleetwood Mac sold more singles than any other chart group in 1969, including The Beatles and The Rolling Stones. As John McVie said: 'We had settled into a certain groove, when you get the feeling that your band is probably the greatest rock 'n' roll band in the world. We had a confidence, a knowledge, a rapport with our audience'.

Even more than *Albatross* and *Man Of The World*, *Oh Well* was Green's handywork. Fleetwood and McVie deserve praise for their superlative work as a rhythm section but in fact *Oh Well* might have been credited to Green as a solo piece, particularly Part 2 where the remainder of the group take a back seat to Green's Iberian acoustic guitar accompanied by recorder and cello. Green has said he wanted to record a semi-classical opus with the London Symphony Orchestra and André Previn. Without going to that much trouble (and expense) he achieved his aim on Part 2 of *Oh Well*. The song was conceived by Green primarily as a performance piece: 'I wrote it as a stage number and then decided to try and record it. Then I thought it would make a good single and they (the rest of the band) made me have second thoughts.'

Actually at one point Green wanted Fleetwood Mac's follow-up single to *Man Of The World* to be Kirwan's *When You Say*. Fortunately the old, pre-success aggressive side of Green's character got the better of his current need to take cover from the limelight. He was so confident about *Oh Well* that he was prepared to put it out as a solo

work if the rest of the band refused to record it as a single. In fact Fleetwood and McVie had little faith in *Oh Well* as a commercial venture and actually bet Green five pounds each that the record wouldn't chart. It was barely in the shops before Green collected his money. As an entity *Oh Well* is the crowning glory of Green's achievements. A brilliant idea is handled brilliantly. In this sense it is illuminating to compare *Oh Well* with Clapton's *Layla*. Both numbers start out with a classic rock riff, then develop into a feast of guitar pyrotechnics before winding down to music that genuinely deserves the much over-worked adjective 'haunting'. Green's instincts about *Oh Well* as a performance number were spot on and when a very different Fleetwood Mac recorded their first live album over a decade later, it was one of the featured songs.

Lyrically, *Oh Well* is archetypal Green – direct and to the point. Green had enough confidence to pursue *Oh Well*, despite the reluctance of his colleagues. The persona Green displays in this song reveals a man almost desperate to put himself down, as if he had no faith in himself at all. Was Green just trying to deflate his audience's expectations? If he was, music like *Oh Well* could only have the opposite effect.

During the band's American tour, rumours filtered back of dissent within the ranks. On their return the gossip was denied by a terse: 'The band is closer than we've ever been' from Green, by now looking more than ever like an extra from a biblical epic with his Jesus sandals, flowing robes, shoulder length hair and beatific smile. Green told the music press that Fleetwood Mac had a busy year ahead of them. He outlined three new projects – a live album recorded at the Ten Party Club in Boston, a Green solo album by Christmas and twenty new songs for the next Fleetwood Mac studio album. He also talked of his new found

Fleetwood Mac receive an award from Disc magazine

interest in religion, an interest that had grown in the hot house atmosphere of America.

He said: 'I spent a lot of time finding out about God and coming back in a big circle where I found the only thing a person could do was good. I had strong feelings that I was walking and talking with God. I was drawing away from the music into just being a Christian person and it made me very happy but it only lasted two or three weeks. Although my faith was strong it was jarred by people who didn't want to know and I made the mistake of trying to explain it to them.'

To disbelieving reporters accustomed to the more traditional fleshy pursuits of rock musicians, Green said he was turning his back on the good life: 'I'm going to stop going to clubs and seeing girls as much as I did because that is a waste of time.' There was talk that he and Spencer would record a religious epic together.

For the moment, however, Spencer was keen to ham it up for the fans by committing his rock 'n' roll send-ups to vinyl. The EP that never was finally appeared as an LP, in January 1970 suitably entitled *Jeremy Spencer*. Accompanying the *Five Foot Wonder* were . . . Danny Kirwan, John McVie, Mick Fleetwood, sax player Stephen Gregory and on banjo . . . Peter Green. Spencer might have got religion but his sense of humour was still intact as these merciless parodies show. Rockabilly, teen ballads, the surfin' sound, blues, boogie and psychedelia are all sent-up with scathing irreverence. No wonder the album failed to strike a chord with rock fans.

Religious experience had a devastating effect on Peter Green's dress sense (left). Jeremy Spencer (right) managed to save his soul and his sweater.

Spencer was playing it for laughs but meanwhile Green's disquiet at being the superstar of Fleetwood Mac was reaching boiling point. Events occuring elsewhere in the increasingly volatile atmosphere of rock, as the Swinging Sixties gave way to the Sour Seventies, were bound to increase Green's restlessness. The painful and protracted break-up of the Beatles, the fiasco of Blind Faith, who split up after just one album and tour, were symptomatic of a new way of thinking amongst rock musicians. Bands seemed to be something from another age. Now was the time for composers and players, ever more conscious of their status as 'artists', to make their own, solo records. *Oh Well* had very little to do with Fleetwood Mac playing together as a group. It could easily have been made by Green and a bunch of session players. More to the point, this guitarist who came from the wrong side of town was, instead of rejoicing in his new found affluence, actually beginning to detest it.

In Green's mind the money now coming into Fleetwood Mac was something to be ashamed of. Before appearing at a charity concert for deprived Jews, he said: 'I want to do it because I won't have to *touch* the money.' In other words, he didn't want to get his hands dirty. Later, he said: 'The very least I can do is give away money I don't need.' Manager Clifford Davis has said that Green told him that he thought it was wrong 'that a group of entertainers such as Fleetwood Mac should earn vast sums of money when,

in fact, other people in the world didn't have enough to eat.' Echoes of Green's mescalin trip where he was tormented by images of starving African children.

Green proposed that the band's profits should be set aside for donations to charity. It was not an idea that found favour with all of Fleetwood Mac. McVie has said that initially he went along with Green's plan but had second thoughts when he realised that Green's mind had been permanently altered by LSD. Typically, Fleetwood was more phlegmatic. He said: 'Pete was desperate to find a reason to carry on the band. It was totally naive, and I didn't want to do it. I was earning a living, and we weren't making any fortunes, anyway. It was a pipe-dream, a sort of "Why can't everyone be friends?" attitude. It was an overture to make himself valid.'

Without doubt Green was affected by the prevalent mood of post-Woodstock idealism, which most rock musicians paid only lip service to. He even talked about quitting Fleetwood Mac to live communal style in Germany. The following summer, however, George Harrison, then very much an ex-Beatle, staged his genuinely magnanimous concerts for the starving of Bangladesh, and true to his words, Green was to give away considerable sums of money over the coming years. In 1977 Green's father put the sum at 'tens of thousands'.

It was in April 1970 that Green made banner headlines in the British music press by announcing his decision to leave Fleetwood Mac. A British tour due to begin on June 1 was cancelled. Green's final gig with the band would be on May 24, at London's Roundhouse. Officially Green was leaving because he felt it was 'time for a change'. The statement continued, true to the spirit of the times: 'I want to change my whole life, because I don't want to be all a part of the conditioned world and as much as possible I'm getting out of it.' Green, according to his colleagues, was already 'out of it'. When, years later, Green broke cover to publicise *In The Skies*, his first album for almost a decade, his statements about why he left Fleetwood Mac revealed nothing, and only added to the picture of a sad and confused figure whose experiences with Fleetwood Mac had deprived him of his desire to succeed and left him bereft of self confidence. In part, Green was a victim of his own celebrity. As Fleetwood said years later: 'He was a classic example of a very powerful person surrounded by yes-men, none of whom, me included, could tell him he was really only talking out of his bottom'. Green's parting gesture to the band he had formed two years earlier, the single *Green Manalishi* served only to enhance further Green's mystique, and deepen the enigma he was fast becoming. Menacing and mystical, *Green Manalishi* was another tour de force from the pen responsible for *Albatross*, *Man Of The World* and *Oh Well*, and as different from its predecessors as each before it had been. The song was 'written out of fear', said Green. *Green Manalishi* had materialised after a particularly unpleasant night terror: 'I woke up one night, sweating heavily and feeling like I couldn't move. I just felt terrible and it wasn't that I was sick.'

The number shows Green on top of his form. He plays and sings this deluxe rock song with the commitment he had always brought to the blues. Observers might mourn his departure from Fleetwood Mac but their feelings were tempered by the knowledge that Green had quit while he was at the summit of his powers. Like so many of his peers, Green was leaving his band because musically he had outgrown a particular context. This was not an end, but a re-birth. Just as the former Beatles were filling the record stores with their solo albums, so too would Peter Green continue to make great music, albeit in a different setting. Indeed, Green's own comments encouraged this prognosis. He said: 'I want to get one hundred percent into music. I want to do lots of jamming with different groups and musicans.'

Green chose to make his solo debut, as

befitted a reluctant superstar, not from the stage of a major venue, like London's Rainbow or one of America's Fillmores, but away from the limelight, playing discreetly in out of the way London pubs. That summer Green re-united with his former employer, John Mayall to play on an ad hoc basis with the Bluesbreakers at the Bath Festival. In November Green released his first solo album, *The End Of The Game*. It was an inauspicious debut, confused and confusing, which, as one commentator noted, 'brings into painfully sharp focus the sudden demise of Peter Green'. As subsequent events were to show, Green had lost his bottle. Musically, he was a broken man.

Meanwhile, Fleetwood Mac had to go on earning a living . . .

ENTER CHRISTINE McVIE ...EXIT JEREMY SPENCER

One of the many support acts at Fleetwood Mac's Windsor debut was Chicken Shack, a Midlands' blues group who took their name from the title of an instrumental by funky, jazz organist Jimmy Smith. Blues groups were judged by the ability of their guitarist, and Chicken Shack featured a newcomer to the ranks of potential fretboard heroes, Stan Webb. This lanky, unkempt figure was no real threat to either Green or Clapton, but his spirited renderings of Freddie King material, and the extraordinary voice of pianist Christine Perfect were more than enough to secure Chicken Shack a following in the coming months.

In 1967 there were rather fewer females playing in rock groups than there are today. What women there were almost invariably tended to be chart fodder, chosen by the record industry more for their sex appeal than for any obvious musical ability. To have a songstress of the quality of Christine Perfect was quite a coup for Chicken Shack. Her 'soft, low, flawless' singing voice left the listener always wanting more.

This remarkable voice was alone responsible for Chicken Shack's only British hit, a stirring version of a minor blues classic, *I'd Rather Go Blind*, first made famous by Chess recording star, Etta James. Unlike Fleetwood Mac, Chicken Shack had to wait until summer 1969 before chart success came their way. By then Christine had decided to leave the band and keep house for her new husband – Fleetwood Mac's John McVie. It was to Christine that Fleetwood Mac turned in their hour of need after Green had left them stranded in the spring of 1970.

It was not blues but Beethoven which formed Christine's musical apprenticeship. She was the daughter of a music professor at Birmingham University and this arty girl learnt to play serious piano. She, like so many would-be rock players schooled in classical music, began to loathe the instrument and all that it stood for by the time she reached adolescence. True to type, Christine and a girlfriend left Birmingham for the hundred or so miles to London in an attempt to impress record companies with their grasp of the Everly Brothers' songbook. She was sixteen.

Her parents were not going to let their daughter escape that easily, and Christine spent the remainder of her teens at the city's art college, eventually leaving with a qualification in sculpture. Birmingham was not immune to the early Sixties' craze for R&B, and its influence around the city's campuses was rampant. Christine was an easy convert, with Fats Domino an early influence. Sometimes she would sing at college gigs with Spencer Davis, a musician who was to lead his own band, the Spencer Davis Group, in the years that followed. Christine's first real band was the Shades Of Blue, who she has described as 'a terrible band'. We shall have to take her word for it, since no record company was brave enough to sign a cheque in the group's favour. They were led by guitarist Webb, who with another member, Andy Sylvester talked the classically trained pianist into playing bass guitar for them.

Some months later, after the band's demise, Christine was working as a window dresser in London when she again met Webb and Sylvester. The two were putting together a band for Mike Vernon's Blue

Horizon Records. By now Sylvester was playing bass, and Christine came in on piano and back-up vocals. Initially the quartet (drummer Dave Bidwell completed the line-up) were called Sounds of Blue but the name was dropped in favour of Chicken Shack, which certainly had a more contemporary ring. At this stage of her 'career', Christine held no illusions about her credentials as a rock musician but she was beginning to develop a taste for blues. 'I certainly had no aspirations as a musician, but all of a sudden I found myself listening to Freddie King records, trying to pick up what I could of the piano player's style.' Technically, a musician with her background had no trouble in assimilating the style, and soon it would become widely acknowledged that Christine also possessed a genuine feel for blues. Indeed as a blues singer she has precisely the sort of instinctive talent that Peter Green had brought to Fleetwood Mac as a singer-guitarist.

Chicken Shack had to put themselves to

the test as a live act. It was not long before Christine and her new bandsmen were in the thick of it, playing back-breaking five-sets-a-night gigs at the Star Club in Hamburg, still in 1967 the ideal place for new British bands to develop their act before facing the more discriminating British audience. Money was in short supply, and in the early days prior to the success of Chicken Shack's first LP, *Forty Blues Fingers Freshly Packed And Ready To Serve*, the band had to cart their own hardware to and from gigs. This low budget lifestyle was not the kind of thing Christine's parents had envisaged for their darling daughter.

'My parents used to worry about me', Christine never tires of telling reporters. 'And I don't blame them considering some of the things that happened. I remember the van broke down and we were sleeping with ice on the inside of the windows so well as the outside. It was all humping my own equipment, sleeping under carpets. It was a very rough life.' In other words, a far cry from the life of laid-back luxury the singer lives today. No wonder she intended to give it all up after her marriage to John McVie in August 1968, the result of a classic whirlwind courtship.

The news that Christine was leaving Chicken Shack, then still striving to build upon their cult following, was timed to coincide with the release of their new single, *I'd Rather Go Blind*, ironically their only hit. Christine's performance of the song was so impressive that although technically she was no longer working, that year she won the prize of Best Female Singer in the Melody Maker's readers' poll. The victory stunned Christine and put the music business on red alert. She was encouraged to return to performing. The following June she released a solo album, *Christine Perfect*, again on Blue Horizon. In the interim, Christine had formed a band and taken it on the road. But

the tour was not a success, having ground prematurely to a halt after a particularly bad night in Nottingham, where Christine left the stage in tears. Later, she recalled: 'The first gigs were diabolical and promoters were naturally disappointed because we were being paid a lot of money . . . My band was a massive weight. As a solo career, it was a bit of a desperate effort.' The *Christine Perfect* album is colourless. A rare highlight is a superior version of Fleetwood Mac's *When You Say*, spruced up by some tasteful licks by its composer, Danny Kirwan. Christine complained that the record was 'a rushed job'. The music business didn't want to listen to excuses, and anyway, this professor's daughter from Birmingam was no longer flavour of the month.

Christine's self confidence was, then, not in the best of shape when she agreed to join her husband in Fleetwood Mac in August 1970. In retrospect, her becoming a fully paid up member of the band was inevitable. Her marriage to McVie gave her an automatic introduction to the band. Already she'd made an uncredited contribution to *Then Play On*. Fleetwood Mac were in America, rehearsing for their next Stateside tour when the decision was taken to formally request her services. The band had spent the summer in Hampshire, recording and considering their future after Green's abrupt leave-taking. Christine was a frequent visitor to the sessions and one of her illustrations was used for the cover of the subsequent album, *Kiln House*.

In the immediate aftermath of Green's exit there was speculation that Kirwan would follow the troubled guitarist's example. But, whatever the truth, Fleetwood, McVie and Spencer were all determined to soldier on. While the rock solid drummer was beginning to exert himself as the group's spiritual leader, Spencer was left with the unenviable task of filling the gap Green's

going had left. It was not a role Spencer felt at ease with. If Fleetwood is to be believed, ultimately Spencer's new part within the band was to cost him his career with Fleetwood Mac. Says Fleetwood: 'Jeremy realized that in the cold light of day he'd have to take up the slack left by Peter. When Peter was in the band Jeremy leaned on him, and he hid his own personality behind some very convincing fronts. Pete's leaving made Jeremy wonder what the hell he was really doing.' The drummer repeated the point when he told Sounds in 1977: 'Christine joined, but Danny and Jeremy were very strongly pressurized, weirded-out, even, by having to take over as the driving force.' Later Spencer admitted how the new situation intimidated him: 'I didn't feel I could do it. All I could play was rock 'n' roll. Peter was a developed musician. I couldn't do the stuff that people now expected us to play. Danny could play but he didn't have Peter's stage presence.'

The fruits of that summer's labours in the English countryside support Fleetwood and Spencer's comments. *Kiln House* confirms Spencer's musical blind alley. He is unable to use his own experience as raw material for musical expression and actually reveal himself in his music. The one exception is *One Together*, a song about his wife which, according to Fleetwood, was cajoled out of Spencer. Even then, the song's style harks back to the kind of bleached pop that dominated the American charts in the late Fifties, Spencer's two other numbers have their roots in the past; *This Is The Rock* salutes the Sun Sound, *Blood On The Floor* is a send-up of Nashville at its sentimental worst.

Kirwan had to bring Fleetwood Mac back to the 1970s, and he succeeded with considerable style. His nicely understated *Station Man* would become a staple of the band's live act throughout the Seventies. For the original, Kirwan shares the vocals with Christine McVie. The delicate instrumental, *Earl Grey* scores another point. For guitar freaks Kirwan delivers *Tell Me All The Things You Do. Jewel-Eyed Judy*, co-written with McVie and Fleetwood, was suggested as a single but the band demurred, which was probably just as well. In Britain *Kiln House* died a commercial death. A single that backfired would only serve to highlight even more the dramatic change in Fleetwood Mac's fortunes. Across the Atlantic *Kiln House* was more generously received, but broke no new ground for the band.

In the States, Fleetwood Mac had no track record to speak of and no expectations to live up to. British audiences still associated Fleetwood Mac with Peter Green, a fact which the band realised only too well. Fleetwood later summed up the situation: 'We sat around in Hampshire and recorded *Kiln House*, and generally felt as if our support had been cut off.'

Christine McVie was a much needed musical and personal asset when she joined the band for their fourth American tour, in the second half of 1970. Her husband has defined the human quality she brought to Fleetwood Mac: 'She's more mellow than Mick and me put together. She has a great ability to accept situations and put them in their proper order. That's her strength.' Christine's stoicism would be of great value to the band in the arduous years to come. Her ability to accept whatever fate dealt out was tested to the full when the following February, Jeremy Spencer went missing in Los Angeles. His on-the-spot decision to throw in his career with Fleetwood Mac in exchange for eternal salvation with the Children of God has become as legendary as Green's own disappearing act.

54

Spencer was ripe for the persuasive talk of the Children of God that day in late February when the plane touched down at Los Angeles International Airport after the brief hop from San Francisco. Fleetwood Mac were into their sixth American tour and due to play a four day date at the celebrated Whisky A-Go-Go. Another four years were to elapse before the band became big business Stateside but they were beginning to win over loyal followers in America. Their post-blues, California-influenced sound, typified by Kirwan's breezy rockers and Christine's effortless vocals, was more suitable for American audiences than the grim relentlessness of Fleetwood Mac's blues period. But Spencer seemed to find it difficult to commit himself to the band's new music. He was always ready to parody his rock 'n' roll heroes but at heart he was a musical purist. Spencer's liking for Elmore James was a serious business and he was more at his ease in the band when they were re-producing the blues. His own music had never developed beyond these roots, and he was well aware of this. An incident after the band's gig at San Francisco's Fillmore West shows what thoughts were going through the young guitarist's mind. After the show the band listened to a tape of themselves recorded when Green was in the band. Spencer later recounted how the music affected him: 'We listened to *Black Magic Woman* and there were some incredible guitar leads. Then some of my things came on and I couldn't stand listening to it. I said, "That sounds horrible. It sounds like shit".' Maybe, to some people it sounded good but how could I go on with it? I just had to leave. I went to bed and said "God, soon, I can't go with this any longer"'.

Los Angeles had long been a stomping ground for all kinds of quacks and religious fanatics. Since the Sixties its streets, boulevards and airport lounges have been ideal hunting ground for fringe sects. Spencer was perfect material for the Children of God, with his little boy lost air and hippie appearance. He'd just left a book shop known to him from previous visits to the city when he was approached by a member

of the Children of God community, who introduced himself as Apollos. Spencer takes up the story: 'Apollos sang me a couple of songs. He asked me if I'd ever asked Jesus into my heart and I told him I had with some Billy Graham followers at Copenhagen about a year previous, but I didn't experience a great difference, so I thought I'd try again.' Spencer claims that before leaving Britain for the tour, he'd asked God 'to somehow soon make a change and show me something.'

Jeremy and Fiona Spencer

58

He had left the hotel in the mid-afternoon. When Spencer failed to turn up for that evening's gig, manager Clifford Davis got in touch with the Los Angeles police. Five days later, acting on a tip-off, Davis, accompanied by two of the band's roadies, traced Spencer to the Children of God's H.Q., a four-storey warehouse in downtown Los Angeles. At first Davis and his colleagues were barred from entering the premises. So Davis concocted a story about Spencer's wife, Fiona being ill. Finally, after a heated exchange, Spencer appeared. The transformation was shocking. The guitar's shoulder length hair, a mass of tight curls, was no more, and, according to one of the roadies, Spencer was 'brainwashed'. 'He was walking around in a daze like a zombie' the roadie told New Musical Express. Spencer had changed his name to the Biblical Jonathan, and had made a clean break with Fleetwood Mac.

Fleetwood had pinpointed the way in which the responsibility of taking over from Green had begun to get to Jeremy Spencer. Musically, he was unhappy with Fleetwood Mac. But there were other factors that were also bothering the impressionable twenty-two-year-old. For a star, he was hung up about the relatively prosperous lifestyle Fleetwood Mac were now leading. Or, at least that's what he told reporters in the mid-Seventies: 'We drove to the Fillmore West in this big Rolls Royce. It was different from the first time we went there. Then the music was really heavy blues. We didn't have much money and we weren't in the best hotels, but it was more real.'

Clearly Spencer was psychologically unsuited to playing a pivotal role in the band. Arguably he'd *never* been cut out for the leading role he occupied post-Green. Fleetwood has said that in his early days with the band Spencer 'was basically very lazy'.

Said Fleetwood: 'We had a hard time even getting him out for gigs because he'd be watching TV or something, and a lot of the time he'd be wearing his slippers and dressing gown when he was in the van . . . Give Jeremy half a chance, he wouldn't do anything. Very dreamy.'

One of Spencer's dreams was to record a religious epic with Green. The project, needless to say, never materialised. It seems that Spencer's own infatuation with the Bible pre-dated Green's. In 1969 he listed 'Reading the New Testament' as one of his favourite pastimes, and it's said that Spencer always carried a small bible sewn into the lining of his jacket. There are no traces of his religious feelings in any of the music he recorded with Fleetwood Mac, but Spencer was much more likely to hide himself behind a clown's mask than reveal his own true feelings in a song. For Spencer's musical comments on his beliefs, we would have to wait until 1972, and the release of *Jeremy Spencer And The Children Of God* (in Britain the album was released in 1973). It was no great record, as the guitarist admitted: 'It's awful. It's horrible.'

In fact, before joining the Children of God Spencer, unlike Green, had not talked publicly about his religious feelings and the effect they were having on his analysis of himself as a rock star. After his 'conversion' Spencer's language sounded uncannily like Green's. In 1975 he told a reporter: 'When everybody is looking up at you all the time it's natural to feel unworthy of all the adoration and glory that's put your way. Originally I tried drugs but it just threw me deeper into the pit.' Spencer says he first dropped acid on the band's second American tour. 'It was ecstasy for the first four hours until I became conscious of leaving self behind. Then it was torment', he said later. To Spencer his drug taking was yet another example of how he had sinned: 'Acid trips and dope, fame and fortune,

pride and conceit and every other sin took hold of me from the start of the material success of the band, like to the point where I was reading all sorts of mystical books. And thinking Jesus was a mystical myth and believing everything I read. I thought I was super-spiritual and a potential Christ! There were many other mind-power trips that I am too embarrassed to discuss. Music was becoming secondary. I was coming first and I didn't even seem to consider others. I was making my wife's life hell, and others around me, though I managed to entertain them sometimes by being "funny".'

62

Ironically, Fleetwood Mac responded to the crisis of Spencer's sudden departure by drafting in Green for the remainder of the American tour. The 'reunion' was hardly less bizarre than the event that had necessitated it. Green refused to play any of the material in the current set, so the band had to resort to improvisation. McVie: 'The whole set was just a jam . . . We'd arive at a gig and suddenly find ourselves on stage staring at an audience without a clue what to play. We were scared stiff.' Green didn't appear to take the crisis particularly seriously. According to McVie he said very little to the audiences, occasionally sideling up to the mike to address the crowd with something utterly inappropriate like 'Yankee bastards', before bursting into laughter.

Meanwhile back home, Reprise Records released the first post-Green Fleetwood Mac single, Kirwan's pretty, *Albatross*-like *Dragonfly*. But not even the publicity surrounding Spencer's singular exit could guarantee Fleetwood Mac a place in the charts. Despite good notices, *Dragonfly* was destined for commercial oblivion.

Spencer has remained on the periphery of the music business since that strange day in February 1971. In 1975 he returned to London and formed an all Children of God band, blatantly called Albatross. Part of their act inevitably included Spencer's tireless tributes to Elmore James, played presumably with a clean conscience this time. Recently, it's been reported that Spencer has fallen out with the Children of God. A friend of Spencer's was quoted in 1982 as saying: 'Jeremy's very bitter about his experience with them. He gave them hundreds of thousands of pounds – all royalties – and never wants to get involved with them again.' Whatever the truth of this, Spencer looks unlikely to ever return to the mainstream of full-time rock 'n' roll.

BAND ON THE ROCKS

By 1971 the British Blues boom had run its course. Some time earlier John Mayall had jettisoned straight blues for arrangements that were as much influenced by jazz. Eric Clapton's long-awaited first solo album, the eponymously entitled *Eric Clapton* (1970) was criticised by those who believed that the guitarist should stay true to his blues roots. When Clapton released the magnificent *Layla And Other Assorted Love Songs* (1971), he again came up against a critical brick wall, the net result of which was to send the guitarist into seclusion for the next two years. The act symbolised the hostile atmosphere many British musicians now felt they had to work in. Lesser talent, like Ten Years After and Savoy Brown, were beginning to realise that a good living could be had in America by playing endless riffs at high volume. Soon this bastard by-product of the blues revival would be known universally as Heavy Metal.

The more discerning, fashion conscious rock enthusiast on both sides of the Atlantic was buying large quantities of records by such sensitive souls as James Taylor, Carole King and Joni Mitchell. If you called yourself a singer-songwriter in 1971, someone, somewhere would at least listen to your tape. Elsewhere, in sharp contrast to the sneakers and blue denims of the blues boom, a new breed of rock star was emerging – glamourous, androgynous and more attuned to the demands of the younger record market, a section of the rock audience neglected by the bluesers in their heyday. David Bowie, Rod Stewart, Alice Cooper and T. Rex were all stars of this sequined move back to more traditional pop values.

From a British point of view, Fleetwood Mac had more or less ceased to exist after Peter Green had left the band. Now that Spencer had followed suit, Fleetwood Mac had achieved a dubious notoriety as the band who hatched weirdo guitarists. In the new musical setting of the early Seventies they found themselves in a musical no-man's-land with their espousal of 'good, honest, musical values', that sounded increasingly like a cry from the distant past. Financially, their best chance of survival was to court the American audience. This is perhaps the reason why Fleetwood Mac took an instant liking to Bob Welch, a young, well-heeled Californian hippie who, over the next three years, would become an integral, if ultimately frustrated member of Fleetwood Mac.

Welch's personality appealed to the band from their very first meeting. In *Fleetwood Mac: The Authorized History*, Christine McVie told Samuel Graham how Welch 'auditioned' for the band: 'Bob never actually played a note. All we did was sit around and talk until dawn, and we just thought he was an incredible person. I remember saying to Mick that I didn't even care what his playing was like, he was such a good person. If we'd hated his guitar work it would have been a real drag.'

Welch was a genuine Californian show-biz kid, the son of media folk. Bob's mother was an actress. His father was a movie producer. His childhood was not a hungry one: 'It was a real Hollywood number, hanging around Paramount studios all the time, my parents throwing giant catered parties, the whole thing. It made me a little jaded and cynical before my time. I never had that real lust to make it – it was almost like coming in the back door.' No wonder Welch has only rarely fulfilled his potential as a recording artiste.

The bulk of Welch's pre-Fleetwood Mac experience was with The Seven Souls, a Las Vegas styled show band who provided ready-made back-up for visiting soul stars like Aretha Franklin and James Brown.

Fleetwood Mac on the rocks. Bob Welch (second from left) was never comfortable with Danny Kirwan.

68

Fleetwood Mac mark five (left to right) Dave Walker, John McVie, Christine McVie, Bob Welch, Bob Weston, Mick Fleetwood

When The Seven Souls broke up in 1969 he and two of his colleagues moved to Europe. Paris and its bohemian myths held a unique attraction for this affluent, young American. There Welch formed Head West, a bi-racial R&B trio. They recorded one album for Disques Vogue before splitting up. Welch was set to return to America, for a job with Stax Records in Memphis, when a mutual friend told him that Fleetwood Mac were looking for a guitarist.

From the beginning Welch was struck by the lax way Fleetwood Mac handled their music. The audition itself was a shock for the worldy Californian, used to a more professional approach to making music. Welch expected the band to tell him what to play. *They* would provide the material. *He* would learn how to play it. But Welch was expected to supply the ailing band with fresh material, had he but known it, a Fleetwood Mac tradition dating back to the introduction of Spencer and Kirwan. Welch later said: 'They didn't talk about direction, except to make it clear that they didn't want to do blues.' Moreoever, their morale was low, and they relied on Welch to restore their self confidence. As Christine McVie put it at the time: 'Bob's like a breath of fresh air because everyone was on the verge of cracking up when Jeremy left.'

Initially Welch did wonders for Fleetwood Mac's music. That autumn's *Future Games* was a much more assured effort than *Kiln House*. Now that Spencer had hung up his plectrum for Jesus, Fleetwood Mac could get down to the serious work of being a contemporary rock band. *Future Games* is a watershed record in as much as it is a complete break with the past. The accent throughout is on an easy-going mellifluence.

Kirwan's *Woman of 1,000 Years* is characteristic, with its sunny, acoustic, Californian feel. The band composition,

What A Shame (a comment on Spencer's exit?) briefly breaks the mood. An uncredited horn player does a credible King Curtis routine, as Welch reminds his colleagues of his R&B roots. The new recruit comes into his own on the title track, a dreamy, almost menacing song. Welch's gorgeous guitar inflections evoke memories of CSN&Y, especially David Crosby's jazz chording.

Future Games looked like setting Fleetwood Mac back on course, albeit in a very different direction. In Britain its release went by unremarked upon, but across the Atlantic *Future Games* broke new ground for Fleetwood Mac by entering the Top Hundred. In performance, the band were also catching on in the USA. An American tour was extended by two weeks. House records were broken on both sides of the continent. At New York's Fillmore East, Fleetwood Mac headlined a bill that also featured the great Van Morrison, then about to reel off a string of classic albums.

The omens looked good when less than six months later Fleetwood Mac followed up *Future Games* with another LP, *Bare Trees*. The album, however, failed to develop the new, softer sound of Fleetwood Mac, instigated on *Future Games*. It's left to Welch's *Sentimental Lady* to make a real impression, and even then Welch would have to re-record the track as a soloist before the number won the recognition it deserved. Christine's songs at this time invariably promised more than they actually delivered. As a writer she needed to relax and become less stylized. Kirwan had no new ideas to offer the band. Even so, in America *Bare Trees* kept Fleetwood Mac's ball in play.

In the year or so that Welch had been in the band he had established a good relationship with Fleetwood and the McVies. He found Kirwan more difficult to get to

know well. A shy, introverted character, Kirwan had remained a mystery to the public since the day he was invited to join the band by Green, back in 1968. He was an unusually gifted guitarist who brought a valuable melodic dimension to Fleetwood Mac. His guitar style was distinguished by an impressive finger tremelo. But, like Spencer, he was hopelessly out of his depth when it came to fronting the group. Kirwan was a sideman who in normal circumstances should have remained away from the spotlight. Off stage he was a meticulous craftsman who spent hours in the studio building up his tracks. Welch has said that Kirwan was 'meticulous to the point of paranoia'. He obviously found Kirwan hard work. Years later, he said: 'Danny was very isolated, very sensitive, and frankly he was very difficult to get to know.'

Kirwan had never been exactly a song and dance man but during the *Bare Trees* American tour in the summer of 1972 he became more introverted than ever. His drinking began to reach unacceptably high levels. Welch: 'I remember seeing him when he wouldn't eat for a week, just drink beer.' As the tour progressed, Kirwan's condition deteriorated to the point where one evening, he was too drunk to go on stage and he watched the set from the audience. The atmosphere became increasingly tense as Kirwan's tantrums continued. Fleetwood told Samuel Graham: 'I was the last mainstay, hoping he would pull out of it. But he just couldn't relax around people, and it made us feel very ill at ease. It became intolerable . . . I finally admitted I couldn't take it either, and I had to be the one to tell him, to put him out of his misery. I knew he wouldn't understand and he didn't – he asked why. It was horrible.' The tour was cut short and Kirwan was asked to leave. Officially, Fleetwood Mac and Kirwan parted company because of 'differences of musical policy'. In the years

that followed, the gifted guitarist has been silent, save for a handful of indifferent solo albums.

On the face of it replacing Danny Kirwan posed no real problems for Fleetwood Mac. After all Kirwan had not left them, it was they, the group who'd decided to dispense with his services, and not the other way around as was the case with Green and Spencer. In both instances, Fleetwood Mac chose a successor who was of real and lasting benefit to the band. Whether this was the result of careful judgement or plain luck is a moot point. But when it came to replacing Kirwan, their luck was about to run out. For even by Fleetwood Mac standards the next eighteen months were to be a particularly testing phase of their traumatic career.

Technically, Kirwan was replaced by two musicians, Bob Weston and Dave Walker. In reality, Fleetwood Mac, true to character, hired Walker in the hope that he would give the band some much needed personality, particularly in the concert hall. Walker was brought in 'as a front man vocalist', according to McVie, something they'd never had before.

Theoretically, there were obvious commercial advantages in featuring a lead singer like Walker, especially in America where his own band, Savoy Brown had built up a huge following playing blues boogie in the heavy metal style of those metal monsters, Grand Funk Railroad. Fleetwood Mac's manager Clifford Davis was aware of this when Kirwan's replacement was being discussed. Walker had joined Savoy Brown a year earlier.

Originally the Savoy Brown Blues Band, they were formed back in the blues boom of 1967, but had failed to make any real impact in Britain. Walker, like Weston, was an anonymous figure with rock fans. If he meant anything at all, it was to fans of Savoy Brown, and most of them were American. He had met Fleetwood Mac during a recent American tour. Walker came from the same sort of musical background as Fleetwood Mac. They knew the same musicians, players like Andy Sylvester and David Bidwell from Christine McVie's days with Chicken Shack. Like Mrs. McVie, Walker originated from Birmingham, where before joining Savoy Brown he'd played with the Idle Race, an obscure but highly rated British cult band. Weston was another Brit. He too had met Fleetwood Mac on the great American rock highway, as a musician with Long John Baldry, the respected English R&B singer.

After touring America in late 1972 Fleetwood Mac mark seven returned to England to record *Penguin*; the album was named after John McVie's favourite animal, which today still remains Fleetwood Mac's totem. *Penguin* was released the following spring. Now that Kirwan was no longer available to interject some melody into the band, Christine McVie was forced into a situation where she had to deliver. In the past the singer had provided Fleetwood Mac with pleasant but unexceptional material. But on *Penguin* McVie emerges as a songsmith to be reckoned with. Her skills are most noticeable on *Did You Ever Love Me*, co-written with Welch. The song is the undisputed high spot of what was generally another ill-focused Fleetwood Mac album.

Those who heard *Did You Ever Love Me*, rightly released as a single on both sides of the Atlantic, might have been excused for thinking that Fleetwood Mac had at last re-discovered their old prowess as a singles band. Inexplicably, this classy pop-rock ballad, arranged imaginatively to incorporate steel drums, refused to chart. Clearly the market was not yet ready for the post-blues Fleetwood Mac. Stylistically, *Did You Ever Love Me* and another of Christine's songs, *Remember Me* (the *first* single culled

from *Penguin*) are very similar to two of McVie's later songs, *Over My Head* and *Say You Love Me*, both of which struck home for Fleetwood Mac on a grand scale. Still, at the time, McVie's songs gave some real quality to *Penguin*, otherwise a rather tepid set.

Creatively, Welch was yet to maximise his potential with Fleetwood Mac, something he acknowledged later: 'For the first couple of years I was in the group, I didn't know what I was supposed to do.' His typically atmospheric *Night Watch*, featuring an uncredited Peter Green, is the pick of his *Penguin* songs. He needed to develop his ideas further. Lyrically, Welch's quasi-psychedelic musings might have been all right in 1969, but by 1973 they were old hat. Fleetwood Mac's new members, Walker and Weston, fail to justify their existence in the line-up. Walker's rendering of the Tamla Motown classic, Junior Walker's *(I'm A) Road Runner* is clumsy and has no case being on a Fleetwood Mac album. Weston contributed one original number, a nondescript instrumental, *Caught In The Rain* that has neither the subtlety nor good taste of Danny Kirwan's instrumentals.

Penguin was received with more enthusiasm by the British music press than Fleetwood Mac's most recent LPs, but the market was too caught up with glam-rock and the likes of Roxy Music to pay any attention to yet another soft-centred album from the former blues band. Nevertheless, 1973 did see the return of Fleetwood Mac to the British charts thanks to a shrewd move by CBS Records, who in March re-released the band's very first British hit, *Albatross*; CBS now owned the Blue Horizon catalogue. Once again the royalties came rolling in as *Albatross* rocketed to Number Two in the charts. As luck would have it, Fleetwood Mac had decided it was high time to try their arm at another British tour. The problem was that audiences assumed that the current

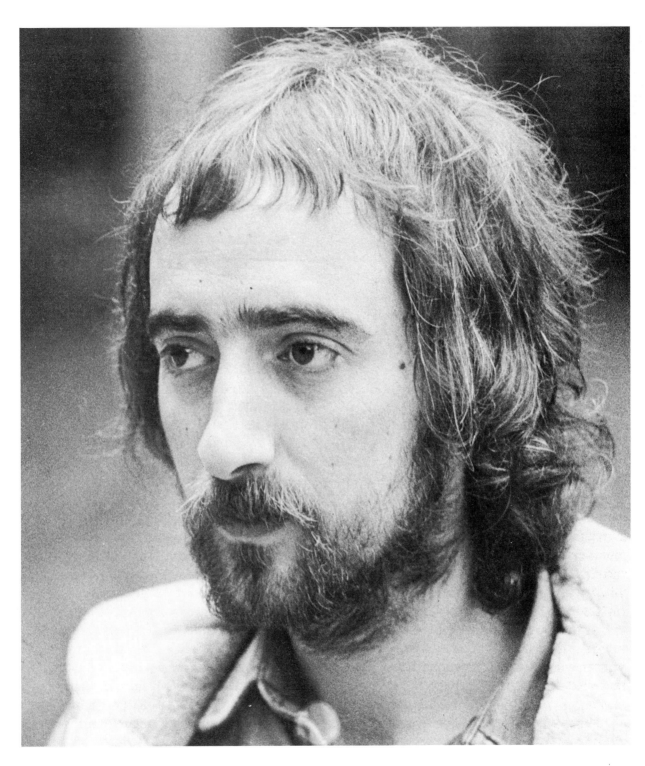

Fleetwood Mac was the same band who had recorded *Albatross*, and throughout the tour the group were repeatedly requested to play the number that still dogged them. It seemed that in Britain Fleetwood Mac would never be allowed to live down their past and become accepted for what they now were – a struggling act still trying to work out their identity.

That summer the band got down to the inevitable business of recording another album. Things rarely ran smoothly for Fleetwood Mac and these sessions were no exception. John McVie and Dave Walker both liked their drink and sometimes they would go on benders lasting two or three days while the rest of the band worked in the studio. McVie was sensitive about his

playing and had to be persuaded to stay and record his parts with the band. Welch has recalled how the bass player wanted to go to France and come back later to lay down his bass parts. Maritally, the McVies had seen more harmonious times. As the sessions progressed it became evident that Dave Walker, far from giving the band a much needed focus was in fact becoming a liability. He wasn't coming up with the right material. Consequently, McVie and Welch had to write for him as well as for themselves. But the problem didn't end there, for when Walker was given a song his instincts inevitably favoured arrangements that bore more resemblance to Savoy Brown than to Fleetwood Mac.

'The light finally dawned on us that we were throwing away what Fleetwood Mac had been, that we weren't Savoy Brown', Welch has said. There was no alternative but to ask Walker to leave and for Fleetwood Mac to make a fresh start on the album. This latest incarnation had lasted less than nine months. The ensuing *Mystery To Me* failed to fulfil the promise of *Penguin*. The fact that the one single taken from the album was a re-working of the old Yardbirds' hit *For Your Love* says a lot for the overall quality of the LP's original material. As a song, only Welch's *Hypnotized* went on to make a name for itself.

If creatively Fleetwood Mac were at an all time low, personal and business problems were about to exacerbate the situation. That October the group cut short an American tour at the request of a distraught Mick Fleetwood. The drummer who normally gave the group its anchor in more ways than one was trying to continue the tour despite the uncomfortable knowledge that Bob Weston was having an affair with his wife Jenny. Weston was sacked and the remaining four decided that Fleetwood Mac should take a long holiday.

Welch outlined the drummer's condition to Samuel Graham: 'He was a basket case, not just because of Weston but because of over-work.' To recuperate, Fleetwood headed east for the African continent, a journey that would have its musical repercussions some years later when Mick made his first solo album, *The Visitor*.

1973 had not been the best year for Fleetwood Mac. In less than six months they'd experienced two changes of personnel. Their career was stuck in a rut. In America they had an audience but other acts, like the Allman Brothers, were beating Fleetwood Mac to the charts and to the stadium circuit. In Britain their case seemed hopeless. On the one hand they were trapped by the conservative forces that refused to accept Fleetwood Mac in any other guise than the blues band of Peter Green days, while on the other they were yet to develop a new identity powerful enough to compete with new heroes, like Ferry and Bowie, incomparably more glamourous than Fleetwood Mac had ever been. Now as a result of personal problems the band had stopped working for the first time in its six year history. In the months to come their mettle would once more be put to the test.

By this time Fleetwood Mac decided to base themselves permanently in America. Mick's sister, Susan later said: 'When Mick went to America he said he couldn't possibly live there. But he caught the bug.' Of the three Brits, Christine McVie now was the most reluctant to give up her English home but she agreed to a six month trial. Later Fleetwood explained why the group moved to the States: 'I'll emphasise that we were on a very gradual up. After *Future Games* in the States at least we began to sell enough albums to ensure that we wouldn't be dropped by the record company, but it wasn't spectacular. The estrangement with England was a very gradual process. We'd gone from being one of the biggest bands to a situation where we'd be either sitting around for gigs . . . or doing lousy ones. We weren't getting feedback from Britain and eventually we found we just couldn't afford to do it.'

But in February 1974 Fleetwood Mac were once again making headlines in the British press, albeit for reasons they could well have done without. 'BIG MAC ROW . . . over two bands with the same name', announced New Musical Express on February 8. Incredibly, it appeared that during Fleetwood Mac's enforced lay-off another band had claimed the rights to the group's title and were at that moment touring America. The music business had known some scams but this was taking rock 'n' roll chicanery to new depths.

Rock bands invariably fall out with their managers. Now it was Fleetwood Mac's turn. Essentially what had happened was that in Fleetwood Mac's absence Clifford Davis had claimed that the name Fleetwood Mac was his and that legally he was entitled to use it as he saw fit. Davis thus formed a new group and called it Fleetwood Mac, regardless of the fact that none of the new band's line-up had ever played with the real Fleetwood Mac. The 'new' line-up comprised Elmer Gantry (vocals), Kirby (guitar), Paul Martinez (bass), Craig Collings (drums) and John Wilkinson (keyboards). Fleetwood Mac's immediate reaction was to serve an injunction that prevented the bogus band from touring. however, although the injunction was successful, the legal wrangling was to continue for some time. Later that year Davis almost stopped the release of the next Fleetwood Mac LP, the aptly entitled *Heroes Are Hard To Find*. It was only after an appeal that an injunction was lifted which prevented Fleetwood Mac's record label, Warner Bros from releasing the album. Later still, in 1978 Fleetwood, the

McVies and Welch sued Davis for royalties they claimed his company, Leosong had owed them since 1973. As Fleetwood Mac's lawyer Mickey Shapiro has said, Davis's action 'turned the lights on for everyone to say, "Hey. Where have all these funds gone?"'

At the time of the row over the bogus Fleetwood Mac, Davis claimed that during the group's lay-off Fleetwood had been to see him with the intention of forming a new group that he would front. Fleetwood denied that anything of the sort had taken place. Davis also claimed that he had read that (1) John McVie was leaving the band and (2) Bob Welch was also quitting Fleetwood Mac, to play with Lee Michaels. Moreover, Davis said that in order to avoid lawsuits from promoters over cancelled tour dates (the Mystery To Me tour) he had had to take immediate action. In the event promoters and concert-goers were put out, to say the least, when they discovered that the band Davis has sold to them as Fleetwood Mac bore no resemblance to the real thing.

For Fleetwood Mac the episode was a traumatic and costly affair that did little for the good will that existed between them and their audience, and which also damaged their credibility with Warner Brothers and tour promoters. If any good came out of the sordid business, it was the decision to let Mick Fleetwood, assisted by John McVie and Bob Welch, take over the management of Fleetwood Mac. Initially, the record company had their doubts about how wise this move was – not unreasonably, considering past performances by rock stars turned businessmen. But in the long run Fleetwood has proved his worth as a manager and would later expand his management activities to include former

members of Fleetwood Mac though not, unsurprisingly, any of the Elmer Gantry band.

The band were confident about *Heroes Are Hard To Find*. In retrospect it's hard to see why. Perhaps they felt euphoric at returning back to work after the trauma of the past year. The best songs are Christine McVie's and it was her title song that was put out as the album's only single. Welch wrote the majority of the material, with an unprecedented seven songs to his credit. Full marks for effort but as Welch soon admitted, Fleetwood Mac had sapped his

creative energy: 'I had come to the point where I didn't feel I had anything else to offer the band. I had just burned it out. Faced with the prospect of making another Fleetwood record, I wouldn't have known what to do. I had a certain type of thing that was liked, but it wasn't any great success. The whole band was just chugging along on one cylinder, and my attitude was that after four years of ups and downs, something had to give.' That Christmas Welch told the bard he was leaving. Fleetwood Mac were now reduced to a trio. Their prospects for 1975 did not look good.

BREAKING BIG – SECOND TIME AROUND

Bob Welch was the fifth guitarist to leave Fleetwood Mac in under five yers. The group had survived Green and Spencer's departures. Now they had to act on Welch's decision to quit. Within Fleetwood Mac there was a lot of affection for Bob Welch. He hadn't saved the day but neither had he chickened out when the going became hard. Fleetwood and Christine McVie have claimed that the Californian was more central to the band than even Green and Spencer. Yet they were too committed to Fleetwood Mac to entertain any thoughts of now leaving the arena, regardless of what outsiders were beginning to say about them. 'Most people thought it was going to be impossible', Fleetwood told Record World in 1977. 'They just said, "You can't do it, forget it. The only way your band is going to make it is to change the name"'. What the sceptics didn't know was that already Fleetwood had an idea about how to fill the gap opened by Welch's exit.

That idea was Lindsey Buckingham and Stevie Nicks, known to the rock business as Buckingham Nicks. Professionally, this bright-eyed boy girl duo were even more hard-pressed than Fleetwood Mac. They had hope. They had confidence, but for some time they'd been trying anxiously to get another recording contract after Polydor's decision not to take up an option for a follow-up album to the duo's debut LP, *Buckingham Nicks* released in the autumn of 1973.

The circumstances leading to what would be such a seminal meeting for Fleetwood Mac were thoroughly prosaic. Fleetwood was doing the round, looking for a studio suitable to record the follow-up to *Heroes Are Hard To Find* when someone

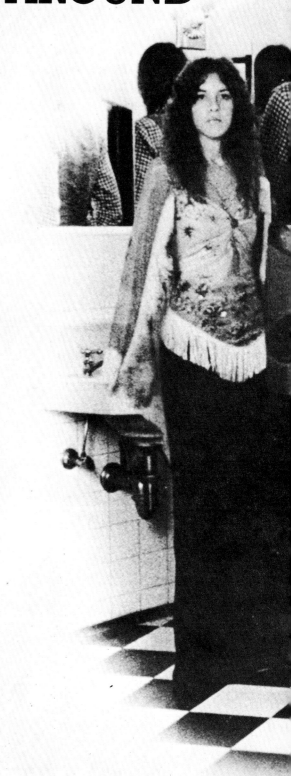

suggested Sound City in Van Nuys, Los Angeles. Buckingham takes up the story: 'So Mick went there. The engineer, Keith (Olsen), to demonstrate the qualities of the studio, played a track of Buckingham Nicks which was recorded there. About a week later, Bob Welch announced he was leaving Fleetwood Mac. At the time, Stevie and I were having a New Year's Eve party at our house, wondering if 1975 would be a better year for us. Keith walked in and said, "Hey, I've got some news . . . Fleetwood Mac want you to join them". You could have knocked me down with a feather.'

Fleetwood offered them the job without even so much as an audition. By the autumn Fleetwood Mac had stopped struggling and were at last back on the charts, renewed and revitalised by the addition of these two youngsters straight from the heart of the American Dream.

Like Fleetwood Mac, Lindsay Buckingham and Stevie Nicks had faith in themselves. 'Stevie and I really weren't that ecstatic about Mick's offer to join Fleetwood Mac because we really believed in what we were doing on our second album', Buckingham later admitted. This confidence was well founded. The songs they were routining for their second album included such future Fleetwood Mac staples as *Monday Morning, Landslide* and the great *Rhiannon*, the song which more than any other established the persona of Stevie Nicks in the public mind. Another reason for their self-esteem was their backgrounds – both came from America's upper middle class. In Buckingham's family high achievement seemed to be the norm. Lindsey was born and raised in Atherton near Palo Alto, California. The Buckingham sons were encouraged by their father, the president of a coffee company, to excel at sports. Greg Buckingham won a silver medal for swimming in the 1968 Olympics at

Mexico City. But there was also time for music.

Buckingham was playing the guitar while he was still in short pants. His elder brother's record collection was a primary influence, and Lindsey remembers his brother bringing home the latest records by the pioneers of rock 'n' roll – Elvis, Buddy Holly, the Everly Brothers, Chuck Berry and Eddie Cochran. 'It was like having the history of rock 'n' roll unfurled in front of me', says Buckingham. But the boy's musical education didn't stop there. There were folk records by the Kingston Trio to pick up on and bluesgrass records whose guitar styles fascinated Buckingham. In the early Sixties Buckingham got into the California surfing sound and developed a taste for the Beach Boys, particularly Brian Wilson's more experimental songs. But at no stage did Buckingham consider the possibility of earning a living from rock 'n' roll. 'Even all through high school, I would go watch bands and even though I played guitar better than people who were up there, I was just doing it for fun', Buckingham has said. Once out of high school Buckingham's attitude began to change and at college he had to choose between ploughing most of his energies into water polo or rock. He chose the latter and in 1967 joined one of the many bands then mushrooming along the California coast. Today Buckingham remembers Fritz as 'a riff-orientated quasi-acid rock band'. Buckingham found the then fashionable acid-rock style too much for his capabilities as a guitarist and he switched to bass. Fritz was still short of a singer so they invited Stevie Nicks to join. Buckingham and Nicks were on nodding terms at high school. Now they began to get to know one another better.

Stevie was born in Phoenix, Arizona but she didn't really come from any one place in particular. Phoenix, like New Mexico, Texas

and Utah, was just another place to stop over while her father, Jess Seth Nicks moved another rung up the corporate ladder. She says she inherited her sense of determintion from Nicks Senior: 'My dad said, "If you're going to do it, be the best, write the best, sing the best and believe in it yourself". As long as I didn't give up on that, it would be OK . . . My dad knew me well enough to know what I should be what I want to be and not complain about it.' Stevie was the only daughter – 'the star in my family sky'. The Nicks tended to keep the girl on a tight leash, especially her mother. 'My mother was very protective of me. All out of love', Stevie has recalled. 'But I was kept in more than most people were.' Later, she complained of an isolated childhood.

Stevie's mother Barbara instilled in her a love of fairy tales and fantasy, while grandpappy Nicks, the black sheep of the tribe, taught her to sing. Aaron Jeff Nicks was a country and western singer who never found his crock of gold. He lived in the Arizona mountains and could work up a sweat with his guitar, fiddle and harmonica playing. Stevie was barely out of nappies when he had her trying out her voice on such country classics as Goldie Hilland Red Sovine's *Are You Mine?*. Stevie claims that grandpa wanted to take her onto the road with him when she was four but her parents put a stop to it. Nicks has never forgotten the old man. Just before his death she put her love for him into song by writing *The Grandfather Song*. The *Buckingham Nicks* album was dedicated to 'A. J. Nicks, the Grandfather of Country Music'. Eight years later *Bella Donna* contained a similar dedication. It is an often voiced regret of Stevie's that Aaron did not live long enough to enjoy his grand-daughter's success and instead died a bitter, unfulfilled man.

The last time Stevie moved with her family was when they moved from Los Angeles to San Francisco. It was there that

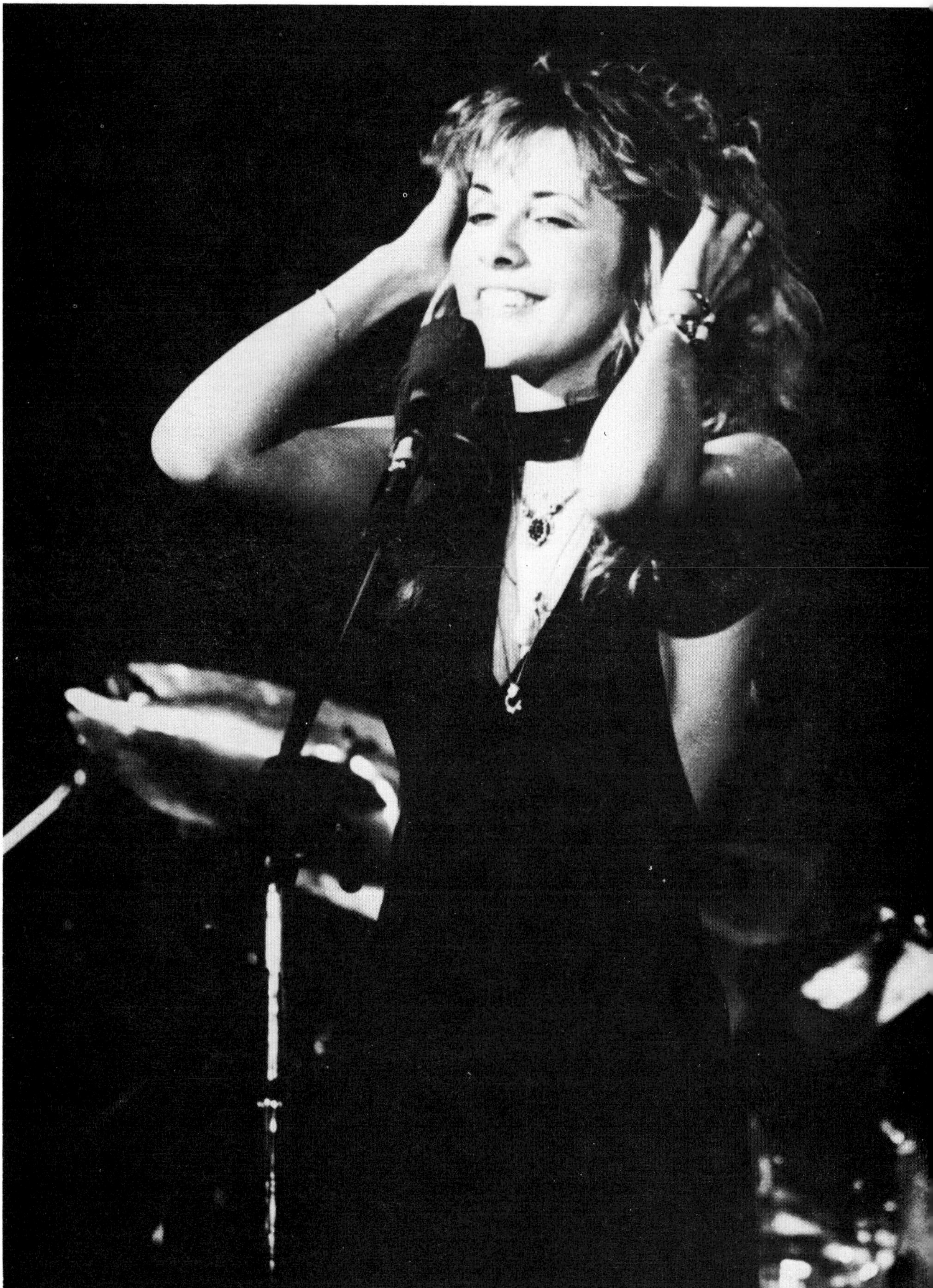

she started to bloom as a woman. Rolling Stone journalist Tim White comments: 'While growing up in the Bay Area, Stevie . . . came out from behind her granny glasses long enough to become first runner-up as homecoming queen in her junior year at Merlo-Atherton High School.' After graduating from high school she read speech communication at San Jose State University, but she dropped out before graduating to join Fritz.

Her musical tastes were typical of the time – the Byrds, Buffalo Springfield and Phil Spector. Significantly, all acts who took great care with their vocal sound. She'd been writing her own material since the age of sixteen. The euphoric harmonies of the Mamas and Papas were another influence and her very first high school group, the Changing Times were based almost entirely on the four-part harmonies of the Mamas and Papas. Fritz were a classic steak and lobster circuit outfit who also opened for the big acts of the day, bands like Santana, Hendrix and Big Brother & The Holding Company whose singer, Janis Joplin made a lasting impression on the eighteen-year-old Nicks. 'You couldn't have prized me away with a million dollar check . . . I was absolutely glued to her. It was there that I learned a lot of what I do on stage. It wasn't that I wanted to look like Joplin, because I didn't. But I said, "If ever I am a performer of any value, I want to be able to create the same kind of feeling that's going on between her and her audience",' Stevie has recounted.

Fritz's manager David Forrester plugged away trying to get the band a record deal and on several occasions he and the band travelled south to Los Angeles to perform before music biz. executives. But to no avail. Meanwhile, Stevie's male colleagues felt increasingly uneasy as promoters and audiences paid more attention to their female singer than to Fritz's music. Says

Stevie: 'The rest of them all thought I was in it for the attention. Those guys didn't take me seriously at all. I was just a girl singer and they hated the fact that I got a lot of the credit. They would kill themselves practising for ten hours and people would call up and say, "We want to book that band with the little brownish-blondish haired girl". There was always just really weird things going on between us. I could never figure out why I stayed in that band. Now I know it was in preparation for Fleetwood Mac.'

Apparently Stevie's ambitious nature deterred any of her male colleagues from attempting to turn business into pleasure. She has said: 'I think there was always something between me and Lindsey, but nobody in Fritz really wanted me as their girlfriend because I was just too ambitious for them. But they didn't want anybody else to have me, either. If anybody in the band started spending any time with me the other ones would literally pick that person apart. To the death.'

When Fritz broke up in 1971 the inhibitions that had existed between her and Buckingham were removed, as Stevie had pointed out: 'We started spending a lot of time together working at songs. Pretty soon we started spending all out time together and it just happened.'

The late Sixties had been a Golden Age for San Francisco and rock 'n' roll, but the centre of the record business on the West Coast was still Los Angeles. With this in mind the couple decided to base themselves in LA. The move was delayed for a year when Lindsey contracted glandular fever but the illness gave him time to hone his guitar styles and for the pair to develop their songwriting. On their arrival in the City of the Angels, they made contact with the big wigs of the record industry. But only Russ Regan at 20th Century Records seemed impressed with what he heard, and even then he had nothing concrete to offer. A more profitable contact was a young studio engineer, Keith Olsen, who for a time shared a house with Buckingham Nicks and other assorted musicians, including Tom Moncrieff (later to play with Walter Egan) and Richard Dashut (now one of Fleetwood Mac's producers). Olsen was to prove invaluable to the duo's career. 'Through Keith, we got a deal with a small label called Anthem which was run by Ted Felgan and Lee LaSeffe, who had previously been involved in White Whale Records', says Buckingham. 'They had a production deal with United Artists. The original deal was for us to go to London, cut an album at Trident Studios. But then Ted and Lee had a disagreement and split up. Which meant the end of the Anthem deal, which had only put out one album, by the Dillards as I recall . . . So we sat around and wrote a few more songs until Lee got himself a deal with Polydor and through him we cut an album, *Buckingham Nicks*, released in 1973.'

Buckingham Nicks wasn't bad for a first trial. Nicks' voice begged attention with its brittle, nasal timbre. There were traces of such disparate talent as Joni Mitchell (*Crying In The Night*) and the English performer Cat Stevens (*Without A Leg To Stand On*) as the pair exploited the current vogue for singer-songwriters. Better was Buckingham's upbeat *Don't Let Me Down Again*, later to re-surface on *Fleetwood Mac Live*. There was no doubt that both halves of the partnership could write effective material. Now they needed to find the right setting. Compare, for instance, the version of Nicks' *Crystal* on *Buckingham Nicks* with the same song on *Fleetwood Mac*. In the meantime *Buckingham Nicks* was left to gather dust in record stores all over America (A British release had to wait until 1977, after Buckingham and Nicks had begun to make a name for themselves with Fleetwood Mac).

Or as Buckingham had put it: 'The record stiffed out and we were eventually back to square one.'

Inevitably, a tour of sorts was arranged to promote the album. In the band was Tom Moncrieff on bass, drummer Bob Geary, (from Fritz) and percussionist Gary Hodges. Their set included at least two future Fleetwood Mac staples, *Monday Morning* and *Landslide*. Incredibly, the only place where the duo achieved any kind of substantial following was Birmingham, Alabama, deep in the southern States. Explains Buckingham: 'We had this very strange localized success – a little pocket of isolated Buckingham Nicks mania. Of the few gigs we'd done, two were in Birmingham, Alabama. The first was opening for Mountain, and the second was opening for Poco. For some reason, we really caught fire in that town. Some disc jockeys had picked up on the album, and it was a huge success there. So we went down a storm. It so happened that our last gig as Buckingham Nicks was in Birmingham. As a result of our two previous gigs, we were booked as a headline act. We topped the bill to an audience of 7,000 and Buckingham Nicks went out on a much bigger high than anyone had expected.

Such isolated success was not enough to keep the record company interested and Polydor dropped the duo after the first LP. But Buckingham Nicks didn't lose their bottle. 'Despite the hardship, we had complete faith in what we were doing', Lindsey has told reporters. 'We had these managers who were trying to get us to do Top Forty stuff. They said they could get us all the gigs we could handle, if only we'd be prepared to play that kind of music. But Stevie and I knew that if we did, we'd lose whatever musical direction we had. And we didn't want to prostitute ourselves so we resisted that and, as a result, got no gigs . . .

90

Nobody wanted to hear Buckingham Nicks doing their own songs.'

Stevie took a job waitressing, for $1.50 an hour at Clementine's, a swish Hollywood watering hole. Lindsey sold ads over the phone for a bogus business directory – and stayed at home perfecting his guitar licks. Stevie: 'I could go out and get a job, and Lindsey wasn't quite as willing to go out and work anywhere. So I figured it was better for him to stay home and practice, because he plays so beautifully, and I'd go out and make the money. If I felt good, I could be terrific as a dental assistant or a waitress. But if I didn't feel good, I'd be terrible. And I'd get fired.'

Later, after she'd made it, Nicks would recall these dark days. 'It's very easy for me to remember having no money. And not being able to buy anything, not even a pair of shoes. That's never left me. It's a part of my life I won't forget,' she told the London Evening News in 1978. Could it have really been that hard for the poor little rich girl? Certainly at this stage Nicks' reltionship with her family was under a lot of strain. When Stevie quit San Jose State to play in a rock band her parents were hardly delighted. Now she was shacked up with a rock 'n' roller and had put out a record with a photograph of her and her lover as naked as God planned, however tastefully it was intended. Stevie has talked about the frosty relationship with her parents, who still had the sight of Aaron Jess Nicks to remind them that they already had one showbiz victim in the family: 'While I was waiting tables, I'd get some money from them here and there. But if I wanted to go back to school, if I wanted to move back home, *then* they would support me. If I was going to be here in LA doing my own trip, I was going to have to do it on my own.' To the Nicks it seemed that every time they saw their daughter she had taken another step down the slippery slope: 'Even though my parents wanted me to do what I wanted to, they were just worried I was going to get down to eighty pounds and be a miserable, burnt out twenty-seven-year-old . . . I'm sure they really would have been much happier at that point if I'd done something else, because they didn't think I was strong enough. I was always sick and I had no money and whenever they'd see me, I'd be really down . . . My father saw me getting skinnier and skinnier and I wasn't very happy. He said, "I think you better start setting some limits here;". They saw in me, I really think, shades of my grandfather, Aaron Jess Nicks . . . '

Once Buckingham and Nicks had accepted Fleetwood's offer to join the group, Fleetwood Mac immediately began rehearsing the new line-up, the tenth in under eight years. Studio time was booked at Sound City Studios. Ten days of recording and the album was in the can. Unlike the group's recent recordings, these sessions were relatively easy. For once, the new recruits had no shortage of original material. Furthermore, much of it, including *Monday Morning*, *Landslide* and *Rhiannon*, was already at the demo stage. As the songs proved, Fleetwood Mac now boasted two fresh, strong writers, in addition to the proven talent of Christine McVie.

From the start Buckingham and Nicks hit it off on a personal level with their new colleagues. 'Did you ever meet someone where you sit down and talk to them and immediately feel like you've known them for a long time?' Stevie enthused. That spring the new line-up played their first gigs. On stage too Fleetwood Mac began to jell. In Stevie Nicks they at last had someone who actively sought the spotlight. Said Christine: 'It's great because Stevie is a show-woman and she loves it. I'm the keyboard player which

keeps me out of the limelight. I enjoy it because I'm not an extrovert.' *Fleetwood Mac* was released in the summer of 1975. The title stressed the group's continuity but musically, Fleetwood Mac had undergone a successful face-lift.

Fleetwood Mac weren't so much transformed as revitalised. One didn't have to listen too closely to hear their blues roots, despite the all-pervasive California glass. Whether consciously or not, both Buckingham and Nicks were influenced by it. The blues were most obviously apparent on *World Turning*, a Buckingham-McVie composition, that recalls the best material on *Then Play On*. The interplay of Lindsey and Christine's voices shows that he can sing the blues almost as well as the former Chicken Shack singer. Note also Fleetwood's playing. For the first time in years he sounds genuinely inspired as two-thirds of the way through, he kicks the song into another, higher gear. Similarly, Fleeetwood is on top form for Buckingham's *I'm So Afraid*, this time employing the African percussion he so obviously loves. *I'm So Afraid* invokes a little of the menace of Green's *Green Manalishi*. The influence of Green is also felt in Nicks' show-stopper, *Rhiannon*, the song about a Welsh witch. It seems that she was more aware of the band's past than is often realised. 'When I first joined Fleetwood Mac I went out and bought out all the albums . . . and I sat in my room and listened to all of them to try and figure out if I could capture any theme or anything. And what I came up with was the word mystical – that there is something mystical that went all the way from Peter Green's Fleetwood Mac straight through Jeremy, through all of them . . . ' Nicks told New Musical Express in 1980. Had she gone back further still, Nicks would have picked up on the similarity between *Rhiannon* and Green's Bluesbreakers' instrumental, *The Supernatural*.

The California effect came through strong on Nicks' *Crystal And Blue Letter*, a song by the Curtis Brothers, given a treatment that would not have been out of place on an album by the Eagles or the Flying Burrito Brothers. *Crystal* bears the mark of David Crosby. Nicks handles the difficult melody skillfully. In the years to come it would be Buckingham whose imprint would be felt the strongest of all. In these early days with the band he appears to be biding his time. Nonetheless, *Fleetwood Mac* shows the range of Buckingham's talent as a musician. As a guitarist he is able to handle rock styles authoratively, as well as the less demanding (for him) acoustic situations. Like Asylum's Andrew Gold, Buckingham understands how to put together an effective piece of pop music without losing any of the more abrasive rock qualities. On *Fleetwood Mac*, Buckingham, and to some degree Nicks, must take the credit for the carefully crafted arrangements and the effective use of vocal harmonies. It's these things that now enable Fleetwood Mac to exploit Christine McVie's songs for all they're worth. Her *Say You Love Me* is a mini-masterpiece, thanks largely to the arrangement. Since her early days with the band, Christine had always been able to write a decent melody. Now this talent had the perfect musical vehicle.

It was one of Christine's songs *Over My Head* that gave Fleetwood Mac their first big American hit, in the autumn of 1975. The number was not an obvious single but after a few plays the song's deceptive melody and shimmering texture became irresistable. The band itself seemed unaware of its commercial potential. 'It was the last track we kept, and we really didn't know what we were going to do with it', Christine told Samuel Graham. 'All it had was a vocal, a dobro guitar and a drum track – we weren't sure what to add to that. So I put on a little Vox Continental organ and Lindsey added some electric guitar, and it developed this really pleasant atmosphere. It didn't batter you. But it was the last track we ever thought would be a single.'

A rigorous touring schedule ensured that the group's record releases were backed up by maximum on stage exposure. Fleetwood Mac were on the road solidly from September 6 to December 22, an experience that played havoc with Stevie's fragile vocal chords. 'I did the most severe damage to my voice then', she later recounted. 'We drove in station wagons all over the States. We'd land at an airport and drive to some college that was way out of town. Sometimes we got lost. It was just hysterical.' The singer and her guitarist lover were not used to life on the road in the same way that Fleetwood and the McVies were. There are stories that prior to the release of *Over My Head* Stevie was seriously considering quitting Fleetwood Mac, apparently because of press comment about her inconsistent singing caused, unbeknown to the scribes, by the problems she was having with her voice.

Soon these efforts were rewarded, as Fleetwood Mac strted to climb above the 250,000 sales level that both the band and their record company had come to expect. It was a gradual process as first *Rhiannon* and then *Say You Love Me* followed *Over My Head* up the singles charts. By late summer 1976 *Fleetwood Mac* was selling with a vengeance. The album's sales caught Warner Brothers unawares and at one time the LP plummetted to Number Forty regaining its upward momentum, finally establishing itself in the Number One position a little over a year after its release. Within a single year Fleetwood Mac sold over three million copies in America, quite enough to make it then the biggest selling album in Warner Bros' history.

LIFE AT THE TOP

*F*leetwood Mac had at last struck oil. In England it was a different story. In fact at precisely the time of the band's long-awaited American breakthrough the London music business was beginning to undergo one of its periodic convulsions. Soon a new four letter word would enter the vocabulary of the British. Before 1976 punk and punk rock were terms without any widely known meaning in Britain. *Punk* was an Americanism similar to the British *yob*, an adjective used to describe particularly cantankerous teenagers. Punk rock was used exclusively by rock writers to describe obscure acts that no normal enthusiast cared a hoot for. After Malcolm McLaren's master-stroke, the Sex Pistols, all this changed. Every parent in the land knew exactly what a punk was, as earlier generations knew how to recognise teds or mods.

The abrasive, super-charged heavy metal of punk, with its street anthems sparked off by an England so obviously in decline, was musically, and in terms of its attitude, diametrically opposed to the new sounds coming out of California. Punk was supposed not to care about anything at all. Actually it cared a great deal, as records by The Clash and The Jam show. In marked contrast, the new generation of Californian rockers wrote almost exclusively about themselves, or at least *appeared* to. From the new, militant British point of view the Eagles and Fleetwood Mac were self-obsessed (just like the punks in fact), narcissistic (show me a pop star who isn't?), and 'out of touch' with their audience. In fact, Fleetwood Mac were very much in touch with their audience, a group of fans created largely by American FM radio stations whose programme controllers wanted to entertain their listeners without disturbing them. It was precisely this sort of audience

that had come to feed off what certain observers dismissed as Hip Easy Listening (HEL) or Adult Orientated Rock (AOR). This audience had grown up in the Sixties with the Beatles, got stoned with CSN&Y at the turn of the decade, and had begun to feel alien from the Seventies' glam-rockers, with the possible exception of Elton John who catered for all audiences.

The HEL audience adored The Eagles with their slick mixture of easy-going acoustic paeans to the Good Life, and their elegant, electric rock. In a sense The Eagles paved the way for the success of Fleetwood Mac, when in 1975 their *One Of These Nights* album smashed its way to the top of the album charts. But for all the Wild West fantasies they invoked, the Eagles were about as anonymous as your average session musician. They didn't have personality. As Mick Fleetwood has pointed out, this was not a problem Fleetwood Mac suffered from. He said: 'Not only are the band visually appealing, but when people think of the Eagles or Chicago they just think of a band. When they think of us they think of real flesh and blood people and not hardened professionals.'

Fleetwood Mac had always been primarily a performing band. Now they boasted a unique front-line that featured two women with complimentary styles – christine McVie the solid, earthy musician, Stevie Nicks a she wolf in lamb's clothing. Nicks played to the gallery, an alluring goddess in gossamer black chiffon and suede, set off with a top hat worn at a saucy angle. As she herself put it: 'The princess on stage is my combination of Natalia Makarova and Greta Garbo and the elegant old rock 'n' roll that I love.' Fleetwood and McVie were the old campaigners who'd slugged it out through many a hiccup these past nine years.

In contrast, the all American Buckingham cut a sleaker figure – tastefully flash. The knowledge that the McVies and Buckingham were linked romantically was a source of endless speculation for the public and gossip writers. And when the news leaked out that both couples had broken up, public attention soared. The PR men could hardly have dreamt up a better scenario. By the time *Rumours* was released in February 1977, the sexual chemistry of Fleetwood Mac was already known to millions.

Work on the album had begun in early 1976. By the end of the summer the group had still not finished the project. They were exhausted from touring continuously, and technical problems abounded as they moved from one studio to another; that the end result sounds fresher and more spontaneous than *Fleetwood Mac* says a lot for the skill that went into recording *Rumours*. But the real hold-up was having to work in a highly charged emotional atmosphere. In the spring of 1976 Mick was divorced from his wife Jenny; the couple later re-married, only to divorce and re-marry and divorce again. Yet Fleetwood's marital problems were as nothing compared to the romantic difficulties his colleagues were experiencing. At least he didn't have to work with his former partner, which was the situation that both the McVies and Lindsey and Stevie now uncomfortably found themselves in.

In the past Fleetwood Mac had had to cope with more than their share of crises, albeit in a professional context. Now business and pleasure looked like seeing them off for good. 'When the shit hit the fan everybody probably thought that this *really* was the end of Fleetwood Mac, and that it would be impossible to work under such intense conditions' – Fleetwood told NME in 1977. 'Theoretically, it was a helluva bad time to try and record a new album, but in

retrospect it proved to be the reverse. Because it all came out in the music.' As the drummer put it: 'We just went through our collective traumas head on and it was then that we all revealed our true colours. In the past both John and I have had to handle some pretty weird situations . . . Peter Green . . . Jeremy Spencer, but as far as Lindsey and Stevie were concerned, they didn't go like lambs to the slaughter, they just underwent a crash course in maturity.' In other words with everything to play for there was nothing for it but to keep their heads down and press on regardless. Christine explained to the Daily Express: 'We had two alternatives; to go our own separate ways and see the band collapse, or to grit our teeth and to stick it out and to carry on playing together. Normally, when couples split, they don't have to see each other again. We were forced to get over these differences.'

Statistically, the McVie's marriage had done well to survive for so long and to endure so much. Christine summed it up: 'As John said, he and I spent the equivalent of forty years of marriage together . . . we just wore each other out emotionally.' Working together had exerted fatal pressure on the seven year marriage, as Christine realised: 'There is no doubt that the band just pulled our marriage apart. We saw so much of each other at work, at play and at home that it became very wearing on the relationship. I used to think that it was more strain on the marriage to be on tour away from home. But not many relationships could survive if they saw each other every hour of the day.' For the moment she and John had to be 'super mature': 'There was a lot of awkwardness, as you can imagine, particularly in the early days after we stopped living together. It was a matter of trying to be super mature about it, keeping our feelings covered up.'

These 'feelings' were, however, explicit enough when *Rumours* was finally released after seven months of recording. The first single, Buckingham's scorching, emotionally candid *Go Your Own Way* is typical. This bitter volley addressed to his former lover doesn't mince words, an impression re-inforced by Buckingham's other songs on *Rumours – Second Hand News* and *Never Going Back Again*. Nicks didn't believe in holding back either as she makes clear on *Dreams* and *Silver Springs*; the latter was not included on the LP but was released as the B side of *Go Your Own Way*. It was as if John Lennon had included his vituperative put down of Paul McCartney, *How Do You Sleep?* on a Beatles album. In contrast to this verbal slanging match between Buckingham and Nicks, Christine McVie's songs on *Rumours* look to the future instead of dwelling on the past. *Don't Stop* is whole-heartedly optimistic and on *Songbird* and *You Make Loving Fun* McVie salutes new love.

The heart and its tribulations has always been the stuff of popular music. On those occasions when the listener can relate the song to a specific autobiographical incident in the singer's life, the song in question takes on an added meaning. So it was with Fleetwood Mac and *Rumours*. 'I'm sure it touched people's sense of romance; people *love* emotional upsets, romantic split-ups', Christine McVie observed to the Sunday Times. 'People were coming to concerts to check out how our lives were on stage – if Lindsey was grimacing at Stevie, or John bashing me with a guitar.'

The public's fascination with the lives of Fleetwood Mac does not by itself explain the success of *Rumours*. There is no magic formula for selling millions of albums, for creating 'mega-success', as the record industry knows only too well. At the end of the day the marketing men can only do so much. Neither is it just a question of making great music, as Lindsey Buckingham later admitted: 'The phenomenon of *Rumours* selling sixteen million copies far outweighed how strong the music was. It's not like it was the "best album ever made" because it sold the most copies. It did well for a lot of different reasons, many, I'm sure, that had very little do with the music', he told Bam in 1980. Timing played its part in the success of *Rumours*, as Christine McVie has said: 'We brought it out when music seemed to be in the doldrums and there wasn't much happening from new bands. Everybody was just waiting for the new John Lennon or Elton John (album). Nobody was coming up with anything fresh', said Christine in 1977, apparently totally unaware of the onset of punk in Britain. In fact, the group had to wait almost a year before *Rumours* struggled to the top of the British album charts, in early 1978. In America its success was immediate and on a scale then quite unprecedented for Fleetwood Mac *and* the music business. Warner Brothers' initial shipment of 800,000 units was far and away the largest in the

band's history. *Rumours* was to remain the best-seller in the Billboard Top 100 for twenty-nine weeks, the longest run at the top of the album charts since the soundtrack of West Side Story monopolised it for fifty-four weeks in the early Sixties. Seven years later sales of *Rumours* are said to be in the region of twenty-five million. A recent survey suggests that as a back catalogue LP, *Rumours* outsells virtually everything else on the market with the exception of the Pink Floyd's *Dark Side Of The Moon*. As Buckingham said, 'the phenomenon outweighs the strength of the music', but just how strong is the music?

Clearly any record that sells in such quantities must have what the industry describes as 'crossover appeal' i.e. an appeal that extends beyond the normal rock market. In other words, *Rumours* was bought and is still being bought by people who don't often buy rock records. This usually leads rock writers to dismiss *Rumours* as adult orientated rock, bracketing it alongside other MOR artistes like Barry Manilow, Chicago, Billy Joel and the Bee Gees, whose *Saturday Night Fever* soundtrack, incidentally, sold on a similar grand scale to *Rumours* in 1977. This is unfair, as the more perceptive critics have realised. *Rumours* has far too much *character* to be written off as MOR/AOR rock. Moreover, like all good rock music, it has emotion, commitment and intelligence.

Buckingham is *Rumours'* driving force. He is able to utilise classic pop and rock styles from the Fifties and Sixties and put them into a contemporary framework. It's Buckingham's abilities as an arranger that gives *Rumours* its carefully textured sound. He is a meticulous craftsman able to bring out the best in his colleagues. As a band Fleetwood Mac sound very comfortable on *Rumours* without losing any of their abrasive qualities. The chemistry that first showed itself on *Fleetwood Mac* comes across with even more potency this time round. Good, strong, muscular melodies and hook lines guide the listener into an album that continually changes its emotional temperature. Buckingham's own, defiant *Go Your Own Way*, an exuberant amalgam of Byrds and Beatles, is probably the key track, but Christine McVie's soulful, *You Make Loving Fun* runs it a close second. Nicks' *Dreams* is pure pop, closer to Abba than Elmore James, but given added weight by the clever arrangement and playing. *Rumours* is not great rock in the way that the Beatles' *Revolver* or Dylan's *Blonde On Blonde* is. As songwriters, Buckingham, Nicks and McVie are too shallow for that, but it is nevertheless quality stuff, painstakingly and lovingly assembled, a mini-masterpiece of post-Beatles rock.

Four major hit singles were taken from the LP – *Go Your Own Way*, *Don't Stop*, *Dreams* and *You Make Loving Fun*. In the spring of 1977 Fleetwood Mac even managed to get as high as Number Thirty-Two in the British singles charts with McVie's bluesy, *Don't Stop*. That April the band returned to Britain as part of an extensive tour that included Europe, Japan, Australia and New Zealand. Three nights at the 18,000 seater Forum in Los Angeles confirmed Fleetwood Mac's new found status. In England it was in the more modest surroundings of the Birmingham Odeon that Fleetwood Mac kicked off their British dates with the 'new' line-up, their first UK concerts since 1973. The band were apprehensive about returning to Britain. They remembered the sustained indifference the British audience had expressed for Fleetwood Mac in recent years. Financially, there was little incentive to play Britain, then in the spikey grip of punk and the new wave. But Fleetwood Mac couldn't resist the challenge. Anyway Warner Brothers'

Burbank office was anxious that the band should re-establish itself in Britain. Said Fleetwood: 'We can't just assume we'll be automatically liked – in the States for the last two years we have been and everyone has known the group and our albums – so it's a weird but really professional ego challenge. But with the group vibe riding so high we can't help but enjoy it whatever happens.' Johnny Rotten or not, the British audiences gave Fleetwood Mac a warm welcome, and despite the wind of fashion blowing in the opposite direction, the band were enthusiastically reviewed. The verdict of the Times' critic Richard Williams was typical: 'They have enough power in the rhythm section to keep a football stadium on its feet, while retaining a reliance on simple, toothsome melodies and driving harmonies.' The Guardian, however, felt that Fleetwood Mac's performance was short on commitment: 'All that was lacking in this clever, noisy commercial combination was a sense of spontaneity and real enthusiasm.'

Compared to their treatment in America the British success was a relatively minor triumph, but by the end of 1977 *Rumours* had enabled Fleetwood Mac to once again become heroes in their country of origin. Ironically, it was early in 1978, just at the time *Rumours* had finally reached the top of the British album charts, that news came through of Peter Green's return to work. The guiding force behind this most unexpected of comebacks was none other than Mick Fleetwood. 'We didn't sit down seriously and talk about management as such. I offered him my services first as a friend, and because I'm really excited about the way he is now. He knows it's no big deal if I do manage him – a far less terrifying prospect than if he was in some office with someone saying, "I'm going to manage you, kid".'

Fleetwood's success as the manager of Fleetwood Mac spoke for itself. Similarly,

Mick Fleetwood and Bob Welch compare beards

two albums for Capitol Records Welch decided to dissolve the band. At first he considered forming another group but wisely, as it turned out, abandoned the idea and instead chose to record a solo album. The result was the excellent *French Kiss* (1977), a major hit in America. Like Fleetwood Mac and *Rumours*, *French Kiss* was tailored for FM radio. As such it was a perfect blend of classy pop-rock.

Mick Fleetwood was crucial to launching this stage of Welch's career right down to selecting back-up musicians for his former colleague. 'I felt Bob had made a big mistake when he formed Paris after leaving us', said the drummer. 'It was a project he had no control over, and totally out of character for him. He'd been through a whole string of managers in his time who weren't at all creative. I was confident I could offer him the proper facility.' Fleetwood appeared to take his new managerial role seriously, unlike say the Beatles whose business skills with the ill-fated Apple venture had left much to be desired. A Los Angeles office was set up under the jokey label, Seedy Management. When Fleetwood wasn't touring with Fleetwood Mac, he'd spend his days at the Seedy offices. 'I'm a manager, but I don't feel like one', said Fleetwood. 'I'm always Mick who plays the drums first, not Mick who manages the band . . . I decided to expand when I realised the office had become capable of doing the leg-work while I was out on the road. It runs very smoothly.' Fleetwood was shrewd enough to see the commercial appeal of *French Kiss*'s re-arrangement of *Sentimental Lady*, the song composed by Welch and originally released by Fleetwood Mac in the spring of 1972, gave Welch his long awaited break in the US singles charts. Fleetwood maintained that his decision to manage Welch was not motivated primarily by the opportunity to make more money. He said he would only

the RAF officer's son had done wonders for the career of Bob Welch. Welch's solo career had been slow to get off the ground. The talented guitarist/songwriter had disappeared from public attention until January 1976 when he re-emerged with a new band, Paris. The project was ultimately another frustrating venture for Welch. Paris, featuring former Jethro Tull bassist Glenn Cornick and Nazz drummer Thom Mooney, seemed to have modelled themselves on the classic Sixties' power trios, the Jimi Hendrix Experience and Cream. As Welch began to realise, Paris had little now to offer a Seventies' rock audience. After recording

99

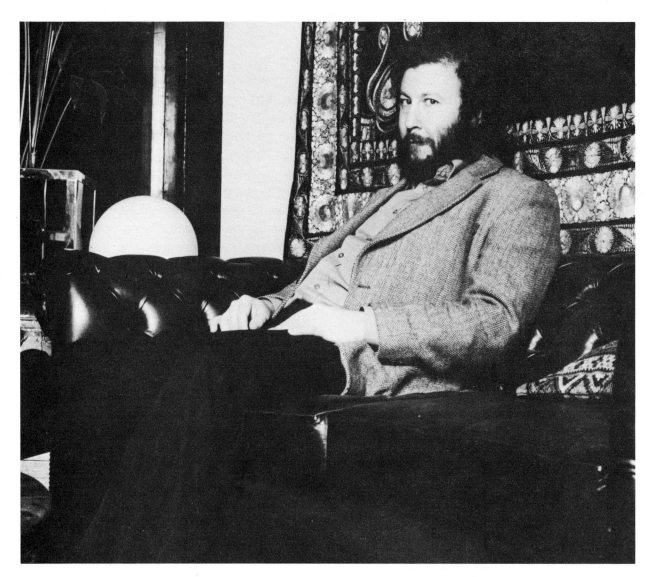

handle somebody's career if it was 'heart-felt'. He added: 'It's important to take care of the essence, and not concentrate too much on the money. That comes naturally . . . Money is great, but it's not important. John (McVie) and myself have been with it and without it, and it hasn't affected us psychologically. It's not what really matters. If it had been, we'd have given up long ago. It's important to retain the right kind of motivation – and the more successful you become, the more difficult it gets.'

Fleetwood's success with Bob Welch had confirmed his abilities as a manager. Turning his attention to Green seemed a logical progression. If Fleetwood could do it for one former Fleetwood Mac guitarist, then why not Green – on paper so much more talented than Welch.

In the 'lost years' between leaving Fleetwood Mac and renewing his friendship with Fleetwood, Green's personality problems had persisted. In British circles Green's strange behaviour had gained him the kind of reputation that surrounded Beach Boy Brian Wilson in America. It seemed that every rock journalist had his favourite Peter Green story. Unfortunately Green's actual behaviour often outdid the colourful musings of those who gossiped about him. At various times since turning his back on the music business Green was reported to be living with a German commune, working as a grave digger, barman, as a member of a kibbutz, employed as a hospital orderly, as a petrol pump attendant and even venturing into the hotel trade. Whatever he was up to, it wasn't making music. Officially Green hadn't entered a recording studio since releasing a single in 1972, the indifferent *Beast Of Burden*, made in collaboration with one Nigel Watson. In January 1977 Green was committed for treatment at Horton Mental Hospital, following an incident with a rifle at the offices of his accountant, Clifford Addams. Green had gone to see Addams armed with a .22 rifle, insisting that royalty payments of t30,000 a year were *stopped*. In court Green's counsel explained: 'There have been some difficulties . . . and his (Green's) attitude is that he wishes to make his own way through life rather than make use of any royalties from his past records.' In court Green said he would go to hospital as long as he was not given any drugs. 'I will go to a place where you just talk, because I don't think drugs do anything', he said. Some months earlier Green had made a rare public appearance, at a lavish party hosted by WEA Records' London office to celebrate the American success of Fleetwood Mac. All of the band were there and journalists at the reception were astonished at the contrast between the new group, sun-tanned, glamorous and obviously prosperous, and Green. The former superstar guitarist was unrecognisable as the handsome young man who eight years earlier had introduced Fleetwood Mac to the British public with the timeless *Albatross*. Green, now in his early thirties, had aged dramatically. A plump middle-aged man had replaced the slim pop idol.

Observers were surprised, not to say sceptical, when in January 1978 Mick Fleetwood announced that he had taken on the role of Green's manager and that the troubled guitarist was now in good health. 'Looking at his eyes, he's a very different person to then', Fleetwood told New Musical Express, 'He's a total pleasure to be with. He's now capable of being objective about all the stuff he's been through. He's come out

of a lengthy process of getting his feet back on the ground. I don't want to come on like an amateur shrink, but I think Peter's recovery is down to the fact that he's started playing again. It's very destructive when you don't play for a long time. He's very positive about everything he wants to do. Peter's not planning to come back like a bolt of lightning. He's playing like someone who hasn't played for six yers, but who hasn't lost his centre. Sure, he's a bit rusty, but he still plays like no-one else. He needs to get down and do some hard work.' Fleetwood added: 'He's in no hurry. He's waited seven years.'

Moreover, Green had got himself a wife, Los Angelean Jane Samuel; the couple had married on January 4. There were rumours that Warners had offered Green a recording contract and that Fleetwood would produce the comeback album. Indeed there was a 'comeback album' but Fleetwood didn't act as producer and the record wasn't released by Warners. *Into The Skies* came out in the early summer of 1979, by which time Fleetwood had abandoned his plans for Green. John McVie explained the situation later that year: 'Mick put an awful lot of energy into trying to get Peter back to work but it was like putting it back into a sponge.'

Between Fleetwood's plan to manage Green and recording *Into The Skies*, Green had decided to work on an album with one Peter Vernon Kall. Apparently Green's mother Mike had introduced Green to Vernon Kall, a relative newcomer to the music business. He owned the small independent label, PVK Records whose other 'name' acts included White Plains and the Platters' Herb Reid. In industry terms, PVK and Vernon Kall were small beer. But Green seemed to like the businessman's way of doing things.

Green told NME how he first met Vernon Kall: 'I was just motoring around doing nothing with my life and my brother said to me do I want to come and meet this guy, you know. And see what sort of . . . maybe I could come on the label. What he said to me, I don't know how much . . . "Come on, it'll secure my job". I think he just persuaded me to come back to playing 'cause I was cabbaging it up a bit, you know. I was doing a lot of wandering, drifting and dreaming.' At the time Green had just released himself from Horton Hospital. Warners had in fact offered Green a contract – $900,000 for four albums to be delivered at Green's choosing, but Green had flinched at that sort of money and commitment. Instead he chose to work with Vernon Kall. *Into The Skies* is a remarkably assured effort from a musician away from playing so long as Green. And in 1980 Green followed it up with another PVK release, *Little Dreamer*, which again appeared to feature Green in confident mood. The validity of these records must remain in doubt, however, since Fleetwood has gone on record as saying that the guitar playing on *Into The Skies* was provided not by Green but by a friend. Fleetwood: 'He (Green) told me that he'd handed over the guitar duties to someone else – ridiculous.' Fleetwood has also cast further light on why Green refused to take up Warners' offer: 'The day he was supposed to sign it he freaked out. I looked a bit stupid. After all, who would believe that he didn't want to sign a contract because he thought it was with the Devil?' Even the tenacious drummer had to admit defeat where Green was concerned: 'I've given up with Peter. Totally given up. *He's* just given up where money is concerned. After a while it just wears me down.'

Meanwhile Fleetwood Mac had more pressing matters to concentrate on. How do you follow up an album like *Rumours*? The answer is, of course, you don't.

While *Rumours* was an obvious place to go to after *Fleetwood Mac*, releasing *Tusk*

was a bit like sticking your head in the gas oven after hearing you've won the pools as the record industry realized only too quickly when Fleetwood Mac informed Warners that they were following up *Rumours* with a double album. 'Doing a double album didn't make any sense at all', Fleetwood said in 1980. 'But it meant a lot to us artistically – whether we could still feel challenged.'

In a sense making a double album is a perfect way of getting out of the responsibility of following up a very successful record. It takes the heat out of the situation by side-stepping people's expectations. The Beatles did it after *Sgt. Pepper*. But in industry terms *Rumours* is a watershed record. Moreover, at the time the record industry was relying on Fleetwood Mac's next album to pull the business out of recession. It was almost as if Fleetwood Mac had set out to be perverse deliberately – and at a stroke upset industry calculations and their fans' expectations.

By the autumn of 1978 the writing was on the wall for the record industry. All over the world record markets were collapsing. In 1979 there were redundancies on both sides of the Atlantic as record companies attempted to cut costs. Growing unemployment had a disproportionate effect on the young. Paradoxically, those in work had more choice when it came to spending their money. Other forms of home entertainment – home computers and video – were competing for the record buyer's pocket. The British vogue for punk and new wave caught the record industry unawares. With its limited appeal the new music wasn't easy to market. As the pinch made itself felt record companies blamed home taping for eating into their profits. In Britain the industry's trade organisation, the British Phonographic Industry put the cost of home taping at between £150 and £200 million in annual lost profits. When solo albums

released simultaneously by the four individual members of Kiss – a grossly conceited piece of marketing – failed to reach their sales targets, panic spread throughout the business's Los Angeles and New York offices. The industry began to look to the long-awaited new album from Fleetwood Mac as a panacea for the predicament of falling sales and lay-offs. 'I think the whole record business is awaiting an album like this to get people back into the stores', said a spokesman for Warner's Burbank office. Another industry executive summed up the situation: 'Where are the new international superstars, the new Elton Johns, the new Rod Stewarts? The industry is desperate for artists that can generate real record-buying momentum. As it is, we're waiting for Fleetwood Mac to come along and pull us out of this shit. It's kinda sick, but it's a fact of life.' Such was the industry's perceived dependence on this one release and Warners reluctance to put out a double LP that initially the company wanted to release the first of the two record set as a

single album just as soon as it was completed. Warners also hired a New York advertising agency to devise a saturation campaign for *Tusk*. The band saw what the agency had come up with and decided they didn't want any of it. Mick Fleetwood was determined that Fleetwood Mac should not be marketed in the way that Peter Frampton had been. 'For pretty obvious reasons we're preoccupied with *not* overselling ourselves', said Fleetwood.

In all, *Tusk* was over a year in the making. This time the group couldn't excuse the long gestation period by offering a blow by blow account of their traumatic love lives. By Fleetwood Mac standards the emotional temperature had begun to cool. On leaving her husband, Christine had had a brief affair with the band's lighting engineer, Currie Grant. The aide revealed all to Rolling Stone, adding the fact that he'd also been intimate with Stevie Nicks. The new man in Mrs McVie's life was Beach Boy Dennis Wilson. Meanwhile John McVie had remarried. But Stevie Nicks' romantic pursuits were still fodder for the gossip writers. Her suitors included Don Henley, J. D. Souther and record boss, Paul Fishkin.

One thing that did capture the attention of the press was the cost of recording *Tusk*. The Daily Mail, rightly or wrongly, described it as 'the most expensive LP in rock history.' A round £750,000 was quoted. John McVie broke his normal silence in September 1979 to reveal to Melody Maker: 'We work in a fairly untogether way, and the luxury of having a successful album beforehand *did* encourage us to take our time.' Originally the band were going to have their own studio built but Warner Bros advised against it on the grounds that it would be too expensive. Ironically, the group ended up spending so much because they used an expensive studio. 'In the context of the whole *Rumours* took longer to make than *Tusk*', commented Buckingham. 'One of the reasons why *Tusk* cost so much is that we happened to be at a studio that was charging a fuck of a lot of money. During the making of *Tusk* we were in the studio for about ten months and we got twenty songs out of it. The *Rumours* album took the same amount of time. It didn't cost so much because we were in a cheaper studio. There's no denying what it cost, but I think it's been taken just a little out of context.' Christine has been less defensive about the expense involved. In 1982 she told the Guardian: 'Recording Tusk was quite absurd. The rider for refreshments was like a telephone directory: exotic food delivered to the recording studio, crates of champagne – the very best obviously, with no thought of what it cost. Stupid, really stupid. Somebody said that what we spent on champagne in a night they could have made an entire album with, and it's probably true.'

Perhaps the biggest surprise of all is the high quality of the net result and the fact that on *Tusk* Fleetwood Mac did not go for the soft option of recording another *Rumours* but instead took a real risk. *Tusk* is not fail safe rock, complacent and predictable. Time magazine got straight to the heart:

'Tusk contains not only some of the most infectious pop music of the year, but also some of the most adventurous. If there was a model or precedent for *Tusk*, it would seem to be the Beatles' *White Album*, an equally ambitious and wide-ranging effort that attempted to bend old forms into new directions. There is much familiar Fleetwood material on *Tusk*, including the gossamer ballads of Stevie Nicks and the afterglow love songs of keyboard player Christine McVie . . . What is startling on *Tusk* is that wild melodic invention of singer-guitarist Lindsey Buckingham, who takes the band off into the ozone on tunes like *Not That Funny* and *I Know I'm Not Wrong*. The title song is

a case in point, released in October as a trailer for the main event. *Tusk*, the single, appeared to go out of its way to shun commercial considerations. It was Buckingham at his most original. In fact, the song was recorded live at Dodger Stadium with brass embellishments performed by the University of California's Trojan Marching Band. Like so much of Buckingham's other *Tusk* material, it was most un-*Rumours* like. Even so *Tusk* gave Fleetwood Mac their first Top Ten single in Britain for almost a decade, perhaps a reflection of the fact that the record shared the same adventurous spirit that marked the best of the British new wave bands.

Generally *Tusk*, the album, was favourably received. Those who, like the Daily Mail, said it was 'bland, often poorly orchestrated . . . that once again demonstrates that endless time and money

do not guarantee great rock music' obviously hadn't listened. The abrasive NME actually bestowed *Tusk* with a glowing notice. Even so, in their public statements Fleetwood Mac went out of their way to be defensive about *Tusk*. Christine McVie seemed to speak for all of her colleagues (with the exception of Stevie Nicks?) when she said the following year: 'I *know* that when you put out a record it means multiple millions of dollars – just like The Bee Gees, The Eagles or any of them. It's huge, huge business, but it aggravates me when people forget that what's behind it is the *music*. We don't consider we've got it all sewn up and that we can just punch out hit records for ever and we'd hope that comes out in the work we do. For *Tusk* it was important to do something really risky, a challenge. Once you get complacent you're as good as dead.' For once, these all too often expressed

sentiments are genuine. *Tusk* is a *challenging* record, thanks largely to the sterling labours of Buckingham.

The guitarist was responsible for nine of the album's songs, compared to McVie's six and Nicks' five. Both women contributed some excellent material (McVie's *Brown Eyes* and Nicks' *Sara* are marvellous tracks and there are others besides) but it's Buckingham who does the pioneering, as the Time critic perceived. On *What Makes You Think You're The One* he is off the wall; his *The Ledge* is crazed rockabilly; *That's All For Everyone* is the finest Brian Wilson music never written since *Sail On Sailor* (the comment comes from an unblinkered Nick Kent in NME). Buckingham, who received special thanks for his production chores, had given Fleetwood Mac another sound. The soft, sweet harmonies were less in evidence, there were peculiar combinations of sound and instruments, Fleetwood didn't always use a full drum kit. *Tusk* is a rich and varied record, an unpredictable foray into pop's outer limits, assured and humorous. It's probably rock's best double album since the Beatles' *White Album*.

Tusk sold a healthy nine million copies, nowhere near the sales of *Rumours* and a figure which fell short of Warner's targets. The music industry remained in recession; the executives would have to wait for Michael Jackson to persuade people back into the record stores. But nine million *double* albums is not to be sneezed at. But somehow Fleetwood Mac still felt they had to justify this LP that didn't take the easy way out. Buckingham: '*Tusk* was very rock 'n' roll and that's the *opposite* of what some people thought, because in one respect it wasn't as intense (as *Rumours*) performance-wise, but it was *more* intense attitude-wise . . . . I don't think people were expecting an album like *Tusk* from us at that point, and the shock probably disturbed a lot of people.'

GOING SOLO

*I*n the immediate post-*Tusk* period
Fleetwood Mac appeared to carry on
much as before. For almost a year they
were hardly off the road. The *Tusk* tour ran
from October 1979 to the following
September. Fleetwood Mac played thirteen
countries in eight months. In June 1980 they
played to almost 50,000 people in six
successive nights at London's Wembley
Arena but this time the reviewers
complained that the conquering heroes
were 'uninspired', even 'amateur'. One
reviewer suggested that Fleetwood and the
McVies should leave their American
partners and instead add their contribution
to the current blues revival.

With the public Fleetwood Mac were still
very much in favour. They had reached that
point where sell-out concerts were
inevitable. Nicks' shimmering *Sara*, the
second single pulled from *Tusk* was another
worldwide hit. Like *Rhiannon* before, *Sara*
made a big impression with the public and
took Nicks a step nearer to the inevitable
solo record.

Sara held a special place in Nicks'
affections, which made a protracted legal
suit challenging the song's authenticity
particularly disagreeable to Nicks. In her
defence Nicks located a demo of *Sara*,
recorded in July 1978. The plaintiff, a woman
from Grand Rapids, Michigan, claimed that
she had written the song in *November* 1978.
Eventually the case was dropped. 'There
were some great similarities (in the lyrics)
and I never said she didn't write the song she
wrote', Nicks told Rolling Stone: 'Just don't
tell me I didn't write the words *I* wrote. Most
people think that the other party will settle
out of court, but she picked the wrong
songwriter. To call me a thief about my first
love, my songs, that's going too far.'

Since her earliest days with Fleetwood
Mac touring had never really agreed with

Nicks. Initially it was her fragile vocal chords that were the problem. 'My vocal muscles got so bad I would have to go to a throat specialist, especially before we played the L.A. Forum or the Garden', Nicks revealed to Rolling Stone. 'They would give me shots that de-swell your chords enough to allow you to sing. But it's not good to get those shots a lot with your chords in that shape. After two and a half hours of singing, you can shred them, truly blow them right out of your throat. The first time we played the Forum, I went immediately to the doctor for all the preparations, and as I was leaving, he said, "Good luck, my friend". I said to myself, "I am in *big* trouble". At rehearsal, Lindsey started playing *Landslide* and I couldn't sing it. I burst into tears.' Her anxiety resulted in a recurring nightmare. She would go on stage, open her mouth to sing but nothing would come out. The rest of the band and the packed auditorium watched in reproachful silence. But the problem improved when a specialist suggested two days of rest after every three concerts and a concerted effort to speak higher instead of talking in her usual husky way.

But other pressures began to mount up during the *Tusk* tour. Nicks had actively sought fame. To some fans Stevie Nicks, more than anyone else in the group, epitomized Fleetwood Mac. But now that she had celebrity, she was beginning to have her doubts about the effects it was having on her life. For a start it was lonely at the top: 'Following an awards show, my brother Chris got in our limousine and came home. And it really struck me drivng home in the back seat of a black limousine I was so lonely . . . terribly alone. Sort of knowing how it would feel to be Marilyn Monroe or something. It was a very strange feeling and I didn't like it at all.' Moreover the coddled teenager had had enough of being the cosseted rock star. Or so she said: 'I don't

want to be so spoiled that I can't carry on my life when there's no more Fleetwood Mac. I don't want to be Cinderella anymore . . . Some people thrive on being a rock star. I *hate* it. I didn't like being waited on all the time, people following me around saying, "let me do this, let me do that". Later Christine McVie told a journalist pointedly: 'I'm spoiled but not unbalanced.'

Indeed all of Fleetwood Mac were spoilt rotten. The money coming in from *Rumours* now meant they could indulge their every foible. There was a full-time staff of twenty-six people. This included a make-up artist, a hairdresser, private secretaries, a Japanese masseur and a smiling posse of karate experts on hand to provide a protective screen between each member of Fleetwood Mac and the outside world when they were touring. From the outside John McVie ('I'm basically lazy, unlike the others. Me, I like eating!') appeared the most overtly hedonistic. He had developed a passion for the expensive pastime of sailing, long favoured by rich rock stars. It seems that McVie was away on the ocean wave when his colleagues, or at least some of them, were making *Rumours*. 'For the last three months of recording I wasn't even there a lot of the time, because I was into this big sailing trip from Los Angeles to Hawaii. Studios actually drive me crazy', he said to Melody Maker. To give John his due, he has said that a man can only have so much deep-sea fishing, diving and sailing. There is still no sign of a John McVie solo album, however. McVie had bought a forty-one foot ketch from the proceeds of the sale of the house he and Christine had shared. He and his new wife now lived in Hawaii. In March 1981 the couple were fined after police found cocaine and three unregistered firearms at their home. The conviction was later quashed after the McVies underwent lie detector tests.

Throughout their seven year marriage the McVies had remained childless. Now in the wake of *Rumours* Christine took the irrevocable step of sterilisation. The irony of this earthy woman depriving herself of the ability to have children has been commented on before. Despite talk of marriage Christine's relationship with Dennis Wilson ended after two years. The couple had been separated some time when the handsome drummer died a most un-Beach Boy death early in 1984 by drowning while diving. McVie's songs are invariably about love and its polarities. She does not have the self analytical poetic head of a Joni Mitchell but her songs always convey a real warmth. Nowadays, Christine lives in a Cotswold 'cottage' somewhere in Los Angeles. Since she broke up with Wilson the public has been kept guessing about her love life. She appears to live alone, apart from the inevitable staff come camp followers. Christine has argued that men are intimidated by succesful, bright women like her and Nicks: 'Look at Stevie – very intelligent, very wealthy, self sufficient, and even though she is also vulnerable and sensitive, it's hard for anyone to get that close to her when she's protected on all sides by bodyguards, secretaries, housekeepers, the works. It's the same for us. People think, "My God, she's so unapproachable . . . ."' Perhaps it's her middle class Birmingham roots but McVie appears to have kept her head while all around are losing theirs in the rock 'n' roll madness. She can be objective about the Fleetwood Mac lifestyle and candid about its extravagances. On one occasion she said: 'We'd spend amounts of money that are almost immoral, and we'd laugh about it. You tend to forget that you've got to pay it back in the end.'

By the summer of 1980 Nicks had sold her Hollywood mansion, a gothic affair purchased 'because everyone else was buying one', and bought a house in Arizona, and a beach apartment at Marina Del Ray. The Hollywood home was 'too big and pretentious', and too public: 'The friends I didn't mind, but to walk into my bedroom from the shower and there's three people there I've never met before . . . Three different times I had to check into a hotel, to the tune of big bucks, just to get away from it all', she told the Sunday Times. On her own assessment Nicks, a Gemini, is two people: 'I am very sensitive and everything really touches me . . . two personalities inside constantly fighting each other. I'm a fairy princess 50% of the time'. While on the one hand stardom appeared to be bringing her down, she believed in her own talent enough to want to work outside Fleetwood Mac. Ambition after all was a family trait. There was talk of a film based on *Rhiannon*, not that Nicks wanted to be a movie star: 'Getting up at 5.30 in the morning and waiting three hours for the right light. It's not the kind of work I like. I'd rather be in a band – to rush out there in chiffon, have that two hours of glamour, then hop on a plane and go somewhere else.' A script was worked on by Nicks and screen writer Paul Mayersberg, known for his screen play of *The Man Who Fell To Earth* starring David Bowie. The *Rhiannon* film has yet to see the light of day. If similar projects are anything to go by it never will.

While Nicks continued to be the focal point visually of Fleetwood Mac, her musical contribution had begun to diminish. On *Tusk* Buckingham wrote nine songs to Nicks' six. Nicks showed signs of resenting the dominant role her former partner now played in Fleetwood Mac's music. In one interview, she said that making *Tusk* was like being held hostage, with Buckingham as the Ayatollah. Buckingham denied the charge but in doing so revealed another

reason why Nicks was feeling sore. ' . . . she wasn't even there most of the time', he said. 'She'd come in to do her song once a week and that would be it.' He added: 'Mick has said since then that maybe I was getting too carried away with some of the music. It's hard for me to look at it that way. It's weird because everyone was very supportive at the time.' It's said that on one occasion Nicks said she would leave the group if the album was called *Tusk*: the title in fact was suggested to Fleetwood by a friend, photographer Peter Beqard who has worked as a conservationist in Uganda and Kenya. If musically she felt squeezed by Buckingham, as far as the running of the group was concerned Nicks felt dominated by Fleetwood. She told a reporter: 'Sometimes I hate him. Mick is very dominant, he's been the leader of Fleetwood Mac for fifteen years. He's the manager, the

drummer, a father, a husband, he's everything.'

Clearly working with Fleetwood Mac was beginning to get to Nicks. In 1981 she told Rolling Stone: 'I was almost frightened when we finished this last one year Fleetwood Mac tour because that's when I decided I had to stop living in the world of rock 'n' roll. That had nothing to do with drugs or anything like that; it had to do with the fact that my life was completely and undeniably wrapped up with Fleetwood Mac. You can call in sick to a job, a boyfriend, even a husband, but you cannot call in sick to Fleetwood Mac – *ever*. If you have that kind of commitment, you can never really have any other plans for your life.' To a British journalist she was more specific. The same year she told the Daily Mirror: 'When your own father tells you you are not the girl he used to know then you realise it's time to

pick yourself up before it's too late. They love to tour and they love to go to parties. But I can't do that any more. Hey, I'm thirty-three and I'm getting old before my time. You can't carry on like that without it taking its toll. If the rest of the group want to then they're going to have to get someone else to take my place because I'm not going through that again. The craziness was just crazy. I got to the stage where I didn't even know my own telephone number.'

When the *Tusk* tour finally wound up with a sell-out concert in front of 17,500 at the Hollywood Bowl on September 1, Nicks, for one, wanted to take a break from Fleetwood Mac. That August it had been widely reported that Fleetwood Mac were 'splitting up'. The press stories claimed the band had told their friends that the current tour would be their last. There was talk of a new group featuring Christine and Dennis Wilson. As a farewell gesture Fleetwood Mac would release a live album.

In December *Fleetwood Mac Live* hit the shops but the rumours of the group's imminent demise continued. In February 1981 there were more stories. An item in the Daily Star on February 24 said that Fleetwood Mac were 'on the verge of splitting up'. The report claimed that Fleetwood and the other four were at odds. Later the New York Post reported that the group had 'fired' Fleetwood, allegedly over 'creative differences' and a loss of income during the *Tusk* tour. This time Fleetwood felt the story deserved an immediate denial and he released a statement refuting that Fleetwood Mac were breaking up. He said the group would definitely record another album, probably in France. *Mirage* was duly released in the summer of 1982. In the interim there was a spate of solo albums from the members of Fleetwood Mac.

What had happened to Fleetwood Mac was hardly surprising. Similar events have overtaken many a rock band from the Beatles on down. It was irrelevent that in the past Fleetwood Mac had survived so much. When personality problems had arisen in the past the individual concerned left or was asked to leave. Now Fleetwood Mac had too much at stake to change their personnel again, never mind break up the band. It is quite acceptable for successful groups to go into hibernation while the individuals work on solo records (often using the rest of the band as backing musicians) in between sailing a ketch or consulting a favoured guru.

But before the clutch of solo albums came

Fleetwood Mac Live, another predictable move and put out, it seems, so hard on the heels of *Tusk* to prove that Fleetwood Mac were, contrary to rumour, still very much in business. At the time Fleetwood was understandably more diplomatic about the thinking behind the LP. 'Fleetwood Mac has never done a live album before in any form of this band', he said blandly. 'It seemed to me that after a year on the road there was no better time to release one.' Fleetwood took charge of the project drawing on 400 performances from over four years' worth of Fleetwood Mac concerts. Given the group's undoubted prowess as a live act and the choice Fleetwood had in selecting suitable material, it's remarkable that the album turned out so mediocre. By including several songs not available anywhere else in the band's recorded catalogue, including a version of Brian Wilson's *The Farmer's Daughter* from the Beach Boy's vaults, on paper *Live* looked a good bet. In the tradition of Jackson Browne's *Running On Empty* not all of the songs were recorded live in front of an audience. Some were recorded privately, either for friends or during sound checks. Buckingham was initially reluctant to go ahead with the enterprise. He knew just how shoddy these packages generally are and the dubious motivation that frequently lies behind them. He said: 'A lot of groups have been putting out live albums recently and I would hate for someone to think that this is just another in the pack.' As is so often the case in these matters *Live* would have been much more consistent had it been a one record set. Buckingham and Fleetwood come off best in this patchy effort. There are incendiary versions of *Monday Morning* and *Go Your Own Way*. Buckingham's charming reading of *The Farmer's Daughter*, a track from the second Beach Boys' album, *Surfin' USA*, is quite exquisite. The rest is forgetable, untidy

and often poorly played. After eschewing the predictable with *Tusk* Fleetwood Mac were now not only doing what was expected of them by releasing a live double LP, they were also doing it without their, by now, customary flair. *Fleetwood Mac Live is* just another in the pack.

Over the next three years John McVie would be the only member of Fleetwood Mac not to release a solo record. Of those who did it was Stevie Nicks who created the biggest stir. But first past the post was Mick Fleetwood. His unbridled energy seemed to know no bounds. *The Visitor*, released in June 1981, was the result of a six week stay in Ghana. It was a unique project and one which took the drummer several months to organise. Initially Fleetwood approached Fleetwood Mac's label, Warner Bros with the idea, budgeted at $100,000. But Warners turned him down flat. RCA Records had the imagination to see the worth of Fleetwood's idea and a contract was duly signed. 'I think people felt I was gonna come out here and record ethnic grunts and groans and put my name on it because I'd gone halfway around the twist, with being obsessed with bein' a drummer', Fleetwood said.

In fact *The Visitor* is a mainstream rock album and anything other than a self indulgent solo record. Neither is it a drummer's album. The African voices and sounds (drums, percussion and wind instruments) are deployed sparingly and with intelligence. Of the ten tracks only two (*O'Niamali* and *The Visitor*) are exclusively African in their inspiration. Fleetwood took two young American musicians with him to Ghana, Cleveland guitarist Todd Sharp and bassist George Hawkins, from Kenny Loggins' band. Ex-Beatle George Harrison plays guitar on a sympathetic version of Buckingham's gorgeous *Tusk* song, *Walk A Thin Line*. Also present, on two cuts, is Peter Green, credited in full as Peter Greenbaum.

It's Green's steamy *Rattlesnake Shake* originally recorded for *Then Play On*, that kicks off the album. And a very muscular performance it is too. Fleetwood obviously had a ball making *The Visitor*. Working in these circumstances must have been refreshing after Fleetwood Mac. The album is a good natured effort that has real integrity, unlike so many solo LPs. There was more to Fleetwood recording in Africa than fulfilling the whim of a rich rock star. Fleetwood insisted that the local musicians were treated justly, as executive producer Mickey Shapiro has explained: 'They've got a Musicians Union there (Ghana), but no active ASCAP or BMI to keep track of music played. So we went to the union and arranged to pay all Ghanian composers and players full scale, whether they were union members or not, and pay royalties on all compositions.' The locals took a shine to Fleetwood and before leaving he organized a concert, the proceeds of which were donated to the Ghanian Musicians Union. Commercially, *The Visitor* was a failure but to date it is probably the most endearing of all the Fleetwood Mac solo ventures.

Nick's first solo offering was a more conventional undertaking. Three years later it remains far and away the most commercially successful of all the Fleetwood Mac solo LPs. The extent of Nicks' success can be gauged by the fact that in 1984 Rolling Stone voted Nicks Top Female Vocalist with a convincing 25.2% of the vote. Trailing Nicks were Pat Benatar (13.6%), Annie Lennox (7.0%) and, most significantly, Linda Ronstadt (7.0%). While Ronstadt appears to have outgrown West Coast country-rock, it was precisely this kind of territory that Nicks so successfully made a bid for with *Bella Donna* and its 1983 successor, *The Wild Heart*. Clearly a lot of care was taken by Nicks and her producer Jimmy Iovine in putting together *Bella*

Donna, which Nicks ingenuously described as 'a chronology of my life and all the people in it'. If there were those who couldn't take Nicks seriously, the singer obviously wasn't one of them. The American public embraced Nicks with great fervour. Her collaboration with the boyish rocker, Tom Petty, *Stop Draggin' My Heart Around* was a huge hit and the follow-up, *Leather And Lace*, featuring Eagle Don Henley, was another smash. Suffice to say *Bella Donna* topped the American album charts. Nicks responded to her success with another choice comment: 'Somebody's waving a magic wand for sure over this whole thing.'

In fact by opting for expensive sounding Los Angeles hip easy listening Nicks couldn't really go wrong. The bill for the session musicians must have cost the newly formed Modern Records a small fortune but getting Stevie Nicks to record a solo LP was more than just making another record for Modern's co-founder, Paul Fishkin, a former Nicks boyfriend. The singer too saw *Bella Donna* as a labour of love. The record's cover, depicting Nicks coyly holding a white dove and wearing the inevitable chiffon and platform boots, was inspired by a dream.

'I dreamed that I saw, against a background of blue, a white vertical line, which was me holding the bird', Nicks told Rolling Stone. 'At five in the morning I called up Paul Fiskin. I described to him the image, which became the front cover, and then the one on the back, where I've picked up the tambourine and the roses, and I'm looking through the crystal tambourine, which symbolises a porthole, to see the sorrows of the world. I love the symbolism of the three roses, which is very pyramid, very Maya. The white outfit I'm wearing is the exact opposite of my black outfit on *Rumours*. Over that it says, "Come in from the darkness".' So it wasn't just another arty shot of Stevie intended to make all those red

blooded American males part with their cash.

The inspiration for the music was more down to earth. In feel *Bella Donna* is closer to the Eagles than Fleetwood Mac, which is not to say that there is nothing to please Fleetwood on the record. *How Still My Love* and *Edge Of Seventeen* are two such songs. The latter might have been really something given one of Lindsey Buckingham's imaginative arrangements. *Bella Donna* is a meticulously crafted, self-conscious rock album that perpetuates the rock star as romantic hero myth that Nicks is so infatuated with. As Stevie said of the song, *The Highwayman* (her description of West Coast male rockers): 'They are the Errol Flynns and the Tyrone Powers of our day. So long as I have to live with them, I try to make them the most wonderful bunch of guys I can possibly think up.' No wonder *Bella Donna* meant so little in Britain. It was precisely this attitude that the new wave was intent on abolishing. Or so they said. In the States Rolling Stone nominated *Bella Donna* one of the year's best albums. Nicks, however, was aware that not everyone shared the magazine's view of her. She said: 'When critics ask, "Is she incredibly stupid?", it doesn't hurt me anymore. They say some of my rhymes are stupid. But I *know* my words aren't stupid, so it doesn't hurt me'.

Of the first batch of Fleetwood Mac solo projects, Buckingham's was the most disappointing. Prior to embarking on *Law And Order*, released in September 1981, Buckingham had produced John Stewart's *Bombs Away Dream Babies* and Walter Egan's *Fundamental Role*. In 1980 he'd said that he was in no rush to do a solo album: 'It has to be done right or I won't do it.' Unlike Fleetwood and Nicks who'd both, in their different way, brought in outside help to work on their records, Buckingham was more self-reliant. *Law And Order*, apart

Buckingham, McVie and Fleetwood wait to go on stage at the Brendan Byrne Arena, New Jersey

from the odd cameo appearance by Fleetwood, Christine McVie, George Hawkins and Carol Harris, was performed entirely by Buckingham. Richard Dashut once again co-produced. Whether it's the lack of working with other musicians or the strain of making *Tusk* (recorded two years earlier), the result is an anaemic LP that lacks impact. For Buckingham, the production is uncharacteristically drab. Moreover, the songs are untypically workaday. There is a bizarre irony in the fact that one song, the countryish *Shadow Of The West* sounds like a track from one of Danny Kirwan's indifferent solo LPs.

Amidst all this solo activity Fleetwood Mac returned to the studio, the first time they had worked together for two years. In time honoured fashion the sessions were protracted. Initial tracks were put down during eight weeks at Le Chateau, in Herouville, France. Buckingham was still trying to complete *Law And Order*, and work on the Mac LP continued over ten months in Los Angeles. Fleetwood later complained to journalist Chris Welch: 'We had to wait around for Mr Buckingham to finish. He was trying to work on a Fleetwood Mac album and finish his own at the same time and it was a complete disaster.' Nicks was another one who apparently hadn't got her priorities worked out. In March 1982 Fleetwood Mac cancelled a tour because the dates clashed with sessions arranged for Nicks' second solo album. *Mirage* finally surfaced in July. The surge of solo activity – by this time Nicks had completed a successful solo tour – ensured that Fleetwood Mac still held the public's attention. In America *Mirage* went to Number One but it was a perfunctory triumph. The vitality that marked *Fleetwood Mac*, *Rumours* and *Tusk* was largely absent from *Mirage*. In short, the 'chemistry' of Fleetwood Mac mark ten had gone awry in a

blaze of egomania. The same thing had happened to dozens of rock groups before. It's that sort of industry. Relatively speaking, Fleetwood Mac were coping remarkably well. They were still working together – just. *Mirage* has its moments and not all of Fleetwood Mac appeared to be affected by the deterioration in attitude. In the past, pre-Buckingham-Nicks era, Christine McVie's songs had often saved the band from disaster. She does it again on *Mirage*. Her songs have never fallen below a certain acceptable standard and the best songs on Mirage are McVie's. *Hold Me*, deservedly the first single, and *Love In Store* are joyous, infectious numbers that show off Fleetwood Mac at their pop-rock best. Significantly, they are the only tracks tht demonstrate any commitment by the musicians to Fleetwood Mac as a *band*. Conversely, Buckingham and Nicks' songs might as well have been recorded by session musicians for all the group identity they portray. The only other material of any genuine merit on *Mirage* is Buckingham's witty *Book Of Love* and Nicks' *Gypsy*, still below par for the songstress; Nicks looked as if she was hoarding her best material for her next solo outing.

If Nicks' inadequate contribution to *Mirage* can be explained by her putting her solo career first, Buckingham's malaise is best understood by considering his colleagues' attitude to his contribution to *Tusk*. It seems that Buckingham's musical experiments on *Tusk* were not always appreciated by all of the others in the group. In 1980 he was asked by Bam's Blair Jackson if the band were in total sympathy with his adventurous attitude, to which Buckingham replied: 'It seemed that while we were making *Tusk* I would be in the studio and do something and they'd say they liked it, or I'd come in after working on a song for four or five days and they'd never heard it, and they'd react well. In retrospect, though, I

wonder how they felt about some of my stuff. Maybe if the album had sold more they'd be happier'. On *Mirage* Buckingham is over-compensating for pushing back the boundaries on *Tusk* by being too conscious of commercial criteria. At least two of his songs on *Mirage*, *Empire* and *Oh Diane*, have all the trademarks of advertising jingles. Even his best *Mirage* material, the aforementioned *Book Of Love* and *Eyes Of The World*, isn't a patch on *Go Your Own Way* or any number of his songs on *Tusk*. Later, Buckingham would acknowledge that Fleetwood Mac had played it 'too safe' on *Mirage*. He told Rolling Stone in 1983: 'We should have progressed but instead we just reacted against *Tusk*. It was pleasant but much too safe.'

Predictably, it was Stevie Nicks who was the first to make a move after *Mirage* – by releasing her second solo album, *The Wild Heart* in the summer of 1983 backed up by another tour. In January Nicks had married Kim Anderson, a born-again Christian, and the husband of Nicks' close friend, Robin Anderson. Apparently Nicks married Anderson, a former Warner Bros. promotion man, out of duty to his wife who had recently died of leukemia; despite the illness the unfortunate Anderson had given birth to a child and Nicks was its godmother. Whatever the motivation for the marriage, it was short-lived and in August Nicks filed for divorce.

The Wild Heart is a mirror image of *Bella Donna*. Once again Jimmy Iovine produces and the personnel is similar, if not identical, to *Bella Donna*. There is even another Stevie Nicks/Tom Petty collaboration, although the new track, *I Will Run To You* lacks the appeal of *Stop Draggin' My Heart Around*. There is, needless to say, some strong material on *The Wild Heart*, most notably the menacing *Nightbird*, the driving *Nothing Ever Changes* and *Sable On Blond*

which recalls *Rumours' Dreams*. *The Wild Heart*, with sales of around six million, confirmed Nicks' credentials as a solo artiste of considerable ability. For all its affectations, the album is immaculately assembled and there's no denying the commitment Nicks brings to her work; even the shop which makes Nicks' boots receives a credit, despite the footwear being obscured by the singer's cloak in the front cover photograph.

The prospects for Fleetwood Mac returning to the studio, let alone the stage, took another knock that year when it was announced that Christine McVie was working on *her* solo album and that Mick Fleetwood had formed a new band. Fleetwood's outfit had its roots in a television appearance he and some other musicians had made as a backing group for Lindsey Buckingham. They were originally called The Cholos but the name was dropped because of its unsavoury connotations; Cholo is a Latino word for peasant with derogatory overtones. The line-up was: George Hawkins (bass, keyboards, vocals), Steve Ross (guitar, vocals), Billy (son of Johnny) Burnette (guitar, vocals) and

Fleetwood on drums. They had already done some dates together and an album was imminent. Originally Fleetwood had intended to once again indulge his wanderlust and make his second solo album in South America (RCA has a studio in Rio) on the lines of the African trip for *The Visitor*, but the plan was scotched.

Apparently the band, now re-named Zoo,

posed no threat to Fleetwood Mac. 'I just can't function like Lindsey, Stevie or Christine', the drummer explained. 'They can do an album and get some session people in to back them on the road if they want to do that. But I can't do that because I can't write or sing. The logical thing is I *have* to have a band.' Zoo's first album, *I'm Not Me* lacked the character of *The Visitor* but Zoo,

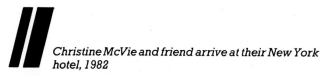

Christine McVie and friend arrive at their New York hotel, 1982

in the words of Rolling Stone, were 'a tight little rock band led by a musician who's as exemplary as he is unassuming.' Again Fleetwood kept his own contributions to what was necesssary; on one track, *I Give* he is absent from the proceedings. Fleetwood appeared to have no illusions about his role in Zoo. He said: 'I suppose my role is to nurture a situation, and to represent something that's musically solid, an entity that people feel safe with. Yes, this is a solo album; I consider it originally my project in terms of pulling people together that I enjoy playing with. And it makes sense to put my name on the cover, because I'm the best known. I would love to keep doing this sort of thing, even if it's not with the same people. I enjoy putting pieces together. I would love to see this become a real band, as I love being in Fleetwood Mac. I love playing live, and I miss it when Fleetwood Mac isn't touring.

For her solo album Christine McVie was taking no chances. Perhaps she was aware of her own limitations and the disaster that her first solo LP had been over a decade earlier. The distinguished producer Russ Titleman was brought in and various star names, like Eric Clapton and Steve Winwood, played on the sessions. But it was Christine's own, quiet dignity that gave *Christine McVie* its quality. Her blues and R&B roots were still intact and visible despite the slick, professional sound. The stand-out track is *One In A Million* on which Christine teams up with another great Midlands rock singer, Steve Winwood. No-one could deny that the album wasn't predictable but after all Christine McVie is the best at being herself. She didn't refute its nostalgic, middle of the road appeal. McVie had grown up with her audience and she made no attempt to keep up with the latest pop fashions. The 'Culture Club types' were not for her. 'You see those people with braids of hair falling down in

front of their faces and think, "God, I must look like a relic from the last century",' she told the Sunday Times.

The album sold well enough wthout achieving anywhere the sales figures of Nicks' records. In the spring of 1984 McVie hit the road with a band comprising Todd Sharp (guitar, vocals), Stephen Bruton (guitar, vocals), George Hawkins (bass, vocals), Ed Quinela (keyboards, vocals) and Steve Ferrone (drums). A review in Variety of her gig at New York's Beacon Theatre concluded by contrasting McVie's style with that of her Fleetwood Mac colleague, Stevie Nicks: 'Altogether, her performance makes for a pleasant, charming show, although it is not comparable in excitement to the galvanizing solo concert here last year of that other Fleetwood femme, Stevie Nicks.'

In the spring of 1984 there are plans for another Fleetwood Mac album. Lindsey Buckingham has his second solo album, *I'm Not Insane* in the can. It's produced by Roy Thomas Baker (Queen, The Cars) so hopefuly it will be a more cogent effort than its predecessor. Nicks is unlikely to end her own solo career and a third LP is inevitable. Yet if Fleetwood Mac are to carry on in any real sense, the individuals concerned must soon make a firm commitment to the band that has in its seventeen-year history survived so many trials and traumas. The man who has kept it rolling for so long, Mick Fleetwood said recently: 'I don't know how much longer we can go on doing these solo albums. It's like a set list that won't end.' The drummer must have felt the irony of his words. For he might have added that either the solo projects are brought to a halt, or Fleetwood Mac drop the pretence and admit that some time back they ceased to exist as a group. Others have thrown in the towel without achieving the twice over success that is Fleetwood Mac's unique and very special contribution to rock music.

DISCOGRAPHY

(Release details are British unless stated otherwise)

Fleetwood Mac

Albums

Peter Green's Fleetwood Mac (Blue Horizon 63200, 1968)

Mr Wonderful (Blue Horizon 63205, 1968)

English Rose (Epic 26446, reissued on Columbia Special Products P 11651, US only)

The Pious Bird Of Good Omen (Blue Horizon 63215, 1969)

Then Play On (Reprise 9000, 1969)

Blues Jam At Chess (Blue Horizon 7-66227, 1969. In US released as *Blues Jam In Chicago*, Vol. 1 Blue Horizon 4803, 1970. Vol. 2 Blue Horizon 4805, 1970. Re-released in US as double album, Fleetwood Mac In Chicago on Sire 3715, 1975)

Kiln House (Reprise 1004, 1970)

The Original Fleetwood Mac (CBS 63875, 1971. Reissued in US on Sire SR 6045, 1977)

Greatest Hits (CBS 69011, 1971)

Future Games (Reprise 6465, 1971)

Black Magic Woman (Epic 30632, 1971, US only)

Bare Trees (Reprise 2080, 1972)

Penguin (Reprise 2138, 1973)

Mystery To Me (Reprise 2158, 1974)

Heroes Are Hard To Find (Reprise 2196, 1974)

Fleetwood Mac (Reprise 1975)

Vintage Years: Best (Sire 3706, 1975, reissued as 2XS 6006, 1977, US only)

Fleetwood Mac/English Rose (Epic 33740, 1976)

Rumours (Warner Bros. 3101, 1977)

Albatross/Fleetwood Mac & Christine Perfect (CBS Embassy 31569, 1977)

Tusk (Warner Bros. 66088, 1979)

Fleetwood Mac Live (Warner Bros. 66097, 1980)

Mirage (Warner Bros. K 56952, 1982)

Singles

I Believe My Time Ain't Long (Blue Horizon, 1967)

Black Magic Woman (Blue Horizon, 1968)

Need Your Love So Bad (Blue Horizon, 1968)

Albatross (Blue Horizon, 1968)

Man Of The World (Immediate, 1969)

Rattlesnake Shake (Reprise, 1969, US only)

Oh Well Part One & Two (Reprise, 1969)

The Green Manalishi (Reprise, 1970)

Jewel Eyed Judy (Reprise 1970, US only)

Sands Of Time (Reprise 1971, US only)

Dragonfly (Reprise 1971)

Sentimental Lady (Reprise 1972, US only)

Oh Well Part One (Reprise 1973)

Albatross (CBS, 1973)

Remember Me (Reprise 1973, US only)

Did You Ever Love Me (Reprise, 1973)

Revelation (Reprise, 1973, US only)

Black Magic Woman (CBS, 1973)

For Your Love (Reprise, 1974)

Heroes Are Hard To Find (Reprise, 1975)

Warm Ways (Reprise, 1975)

Over My Head (Reprise, 1976)

Rhiannon (Reprise, 1976)

Albatross (Epic, 1976, US only)

Say You Love Me (Reprise, 1976)

Go Your Own Way (Reprise, 1976)

Dreams (Warner Bros., 1977)

Don't Stop (Warner Bros., 1977)

You Make Loving Fun (Warner Bros.,1977)

Tusk (Warner Bros., 1979)

Sara (Warner Bros., 1979)

It's Not That Funny (Warner Bros., 1980)

Think About Me (Warner Bros., 1980)

Hold Me (Warner Bros., 1982)

Gypsy (Warner Bros., 1982)

Oh Diane (Warner Bros., 1982)

Can't Go Back (Warner Bros., 1982)

Lindsey Buckingham Albums

Law And Order (Mercury 6302 167, 1981)
I'm Not Insane (Mercury, 1984)

Buckingham-Nicks

Albums

Buckingham-Nicks (Polydor D 5058, 1973, US only. Released in UK, Polydor 2391093, 1977)

Mick Fleetwood

Albums

The Visitor (RCA LO 5044, 1981)
I'm Not Me (RCA PL 84652, 1983)

Peter Green

Albums

The End Of The Game (Reprise RSLP 9006, 1970)
In The Skies (PVK, 1979)
Little Dreamer (PVK, 1980)
Blue Guitar (Creole, 1981)
Watcha Gonna Do (PVK, 1981)
White Sky (PVK, 1982)
Kolors (PVK, 1983)

Danny Kirwan

Albums

Second Chapter (DJM DJF 20454, 1975)
Midnight In San Juan (DJM DJF 20481, 1976)
Hello There, Big Boy (DJM, 1979)

Christine McVie

Albums

Christine Perfect (Blue Horizon 63860, 1970. In US released as The Legendary Christine Perfect, Sire 6022, 1977)
Christine Perfect (Warner Bros. 925059-1, 1984)

Stevie Nicks

Albums

Bella Donna (Modern WEA 999169, 1981)
The Wild Heart (Modern WEA 25 0071-1, 1983)

Jeremy Spencer

Albums

Jeremy Spencer (Reprise 9002, 1970)
Jeremy Spencer And The Children Of God (CBS 69046, 1973)
Flee (Atlantic, SD-19236, 1979)

Bob Welch
(Albums) – with Paris.

Paris (Capitol ST 11464, 1976)
Big Towne 2061 (Capital ST 11560, 1976)

Solo

French Kiss (Capitol CL 15951, 1977)
Three Hearts (Capitol EAST 11907, 1979)
The Other One (Capital EST 2017, 1980)
Man Overboard (Capitol SOO-12107, 1980, US release)
Bob Welch (RCA LP 6019, 1982)

Others

John Mayall's Bluesbreakers: John Mayall Plays John Mayall (Decca 4680, 1965) (featuring John McVie)
Blues Breakers (Decca 4804, 1966) (featuring John McVie)
A Hard Road (Decca 4853, 1967) (featuring Peter Green and John McVie)
Crusade (Decca 4890, 1967) (featuring John McVie)

Chicken Shack (featuring Christine Perfect): Forty Blue Fingers Freshly Packed And Ready To Serve (Blue Horizon 63203, 1968)
OK Ken (Blue Horizon 63209, 1969)

PROTEUS ROCKS

The Best Rock 'n' Roll Reading from Proteus

☐ **TOYAH**
An illustrated fan's eyeview
much-liked by Toyah herself.
by Gaynor Evans
UK £1.95
US $3.95

☐ **REGGAE: DEEP ROOTS MUSIC**
The definitive history of reggae.
A major TV tie-in.
by Howard Johnson and Jim Pines
UK £5.95
US $10.95

☐ **BOOKENDS**
The first full study of Simon
and Garfunkel, their joint and
solo careers.
by Patrick Humphries
UK £5.95
US $10.95

☐ **PRETENDERS**
The first full study of this
powerful and turbulent band.
by Chris Salewicz
UK £3.95
US $7.95

☐ **LOU REED**
A definitive profile of this
almost reclusive figure.
by Diana Clapton
UK £4.95
US $9.95.

☐ **JAMES LAST**
A fully illustrated study of this
world phenomenon of
popular music.
by Howard Elson
UK £4.95
US $9.95

☐ **RARE RECORDS**
A complete illustrated guide
to wax trash and vinyl
treasures.
by Tom Hibbert
UK £4.95
US $9.95

☐ **THE PERFECT COLLECTION**
The 200 greatest albums, the
100 greatest singles selected
and discussed by leading rock
journalists.
Edited by Tom Hibbert
UK £4.95
US $9.95

☐ **EARLY ROCKERS**
All the seminal figures of rock
'n' roll:
Berry, Little Richard, Jerry Lee,
Presley et al.
by Howard Elson
UK £4.95
US $9.95

KATE BUSH ☐
Complete illustrated story of
this unique artist.
by Paul Kerton
UK £3.95
US $7.95

BLACK SABBATH ☐
Heavy Metal Superstars.
by Chris Welch
UK £4.95
US $9.95

A-Z OF ROCK GUITARISTS ☐
First illustrated encyclopaedia
of guitar greats.
by Chris Charlesworth
UK £5.95
US $10.95

A-Z OF ROCK DRUMMERS ☐
Over 300 great drummers in
this companion to ROCK
GUITARISTS.
by Harry Shapiro
UK £5.95
US $10.95

CHUCK BERRY ☐
The definitive biography of
the original Mr Rock 'n' Roll.
by Krista Reese
UK £4.95
US $8.95

A CASE OF MADNESS ☐
A big illustrated guide for
fans of this insane band.
by Mark Williams
UK only £1.95

TALKING HEADS ☐
The only illustrated book
about one of the most
innovative bands of the 70s
and 80s.
by Krista Reese
UK £4.95
US $9.95

DURAN DURAN ☐
The best-selling illustrated
biography.
UK £1.95
US $3.95

A TOURIST'S GUIDE TO JAPAN ☐
Beautifully illustrated study
of Sylvian and his colleagues.
by Arthur A. Pitt.
UK £1.95
US $3.95

ILLUSTRATED POP QUIZ ☐
Over 400 impossible questions
for pop geniuses only.
by Dafydd Rees and Barry
Lazell
UK £2.95
US $5.95

order form overleaf